D1534795

Heroes of the
UNDERGROUND
RAILROAD
Around
WASHINGTON, D.C.

Heroes of the
UNDERGROUND
RAILROAD
— *Around* —
WASHINGTON, D.C.

JENNY MASUR

Foreword by Stanley Harrold
Author of *Subversives: Antislavery Community in Washington, D.C., 1828–1865*

THE
History
PRESS

Published by The History Press
Charleston, SC
www.historypress.com

Copyright © 2019 by Jenny Masur
All rights reserved

Front cover: Library of Congress; *left inset*: Library of Congress;
right inset: New York Public Library.
Back cover, left: Library of Congress; *right*: Library of Congress.

First published 2019

ISBN 9781625859754

Library of Congress Control Number: 2018959012

Notice: The information in this book is true and complete to the best of our knowledge. It is offered without guarantee on the part of the author or The History Press. The author and The History Press disclaim all liability in connection with the use of this book.

*To independent and local historians
who research the resistance to slavery through flight*

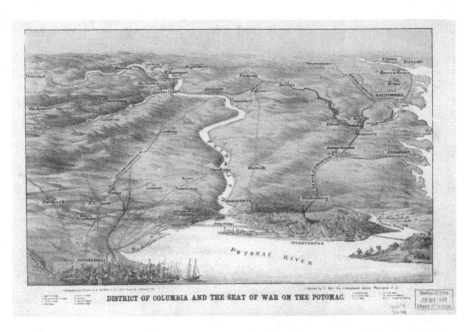

"District of Columbia and the Seat of War on the Potomac" provides a bird's-eye view of the area. Bohn Casimir, E. Sachse & Co. 1861. *Library of Congress.*

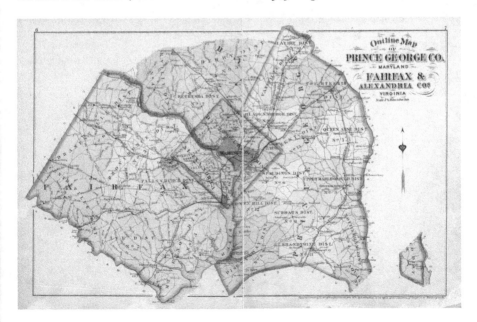

"Outline Map of Prince George [sic] Co., Maryland, Fairfax & Alexandria Cos, Virginia," 1878 shows much of the D.C. region. *Library of Congress.*

CONTENTS

CONTENTS

FOREWORD

An especially brutal form of slavery, known as chattel slavery, developed in Great Britain's North American colonies during the seventeenth and eighteenth centuries. Unlike the forms of slavery that had existed in Africa and Europe since ancient times, chattel slavery reduced those who were enslaved to the legal status of barnyard animals. They had no conventional human rights and could be bought and sold at their owner's pleasure. Also, unlike slavery in Africa and Europe, slavery in America was based on race. Only people of African and American Indian descent could legally be held as slaves, and most of them were African Americans.

When in 1776 the Continental Congress declared the United States to be independent of Britain, it also declared "that all men are created equal, that they are endowed by their Creator with certain unalienable rights, that among these are life, liberty, and the pursuit of happiness." When slaveholder Thomas Jefferson wrote these words, however, he meant that only white men were equal and had rights, and other advocates of independence agreed. In the U.S. Constitution, drafted in 1787 by a national convention held in Philadelphia, and in the Bill of Rights, added to the Constitution by amendment in 1791, the same assumption about who had rights remained in force. The Constitution also explicitly supported slavery by providing for the return of slaves who escaped from one state to another, by extending the legality of the Atlantic slave trade for another twenty years and by recognizing the power of the national government to put down revolts in the states.

In contrast to Jefferson, the great majority of the country's other political leaders, and white Americans in general, a few people, centered in the Northeast, interpreted the Declaration of Independence's equal rights doctrine more broadly. Among them were African American leaders and white supporters of a fledgling movement to abolish slavery. Working in separate organizations, these two groups had a major role in bringing about either immediate abolition or gradual abolition of slavery in the northeastern states between 1781 and 1804. In response, Jefferson, James Madison and other southern leaders insisted that the permanent national capital be established on the banks of the Potomac River, which flowed between the slave-labor states of Maryland and Virginia.

Therefore, the creation of the City of Washington in the District of Columbia, cut out of these states and where slavery remained legal, amounted to national recognition of slavery's respectability as well as of the power of slaveholders. Most other western nations abolished slavery in the early 1800s, but the United States retained this oppressive system of unfree labor and race control. South and west of the Ohio River, the government encouraged the system's territorial expansion.

Yet, locating the national capital on the Potomac also gave abolitionists an opening wedge into the slave-labor South. Starting in the 1810s, abolitionists from the North visited Washington to observe the brutality of the city's slave trade and to interact with local African Americans, both slave and free. By the late 1820s, abolitionists had also organized petitioning campaigns designed to raise in Congress the issues of ending slavery and the slave trade in the District of Columbia as well as to encourage debate concerning the morality of slavery. By the mid-1830s, as abolitionists began to demand immediate emancipation of all slaves, lobbyists representing the movement had begun to interact with northern congressman such as John Quincy Adams of Massachusetts. A few of these congressmen were themselves immediate abolitionists. But most often, like Adams, they actively opposed only the existence of slavery in the district, slavery's westward expansion and U.S. annexation of the huge slaveholding Republic of Texas. These congressmen's ties to the much more radical abolitionists nevertheless angered their proslavery counterparts and nearly all white residents of the district.

This fraught environment in the national capital is the stage of the individual stories Jenny Masur tells about slaves' efforts to gain freedom and about the free people, black and white, who assisted them in their quest. Most of Masur's subjects took action for freedom in Washington's vicinity, including portions of Maryland and Virginia. Their stories cover a period stretching from the early 1820s to the end of the Civil War in 1865. Some of these stories have been related previously, but in a quite different style from Masur's and without many of the details she provides about individuals' backgrounds, desires and emotions. Masur is not interested in general abolitionist and antislavery strategies. Rather, she provides intimate portraits of human beings struggling to escape from slavery and those who took risks to help them reach that goal.

Stanley Harrold, PhD

PREFACE

P eople commonly associate the names of Frederick Douglass and Harriet
Tubman with the Underground Railroad. Frederick Douglass was a
freedom seeker from the Eastern Shore of Maryland who became a
famous orator and statesman, perhaps the most famous African American
leader of the nineteenth century. He was self-educated during slavery and
rose to become a renowned lecturer, newspaper editor and autobiographer,
as well as recipient of appointments as consul in Haiti and D.C. Marshal.
Also from the Eastern Shore, Harriet Tubman is known for her brave
escape and her multiple journeys back into slave territory to lead others out
of Maryland. Less well known is her later career as Civil War nurse and
scout and her role as a humanitarian caring for older African Americans in
Auburn, New York. Both figures are commemorated nationally, one by the
Frederick Douglass National Historic Site in D.C. and the other by Harriet
Tubman Underground Railroad National Historical Park in Cambridge,
Maryland. Both heroes are celebrated during Black History Month, and
there is a Harriet Tubman Day in Maryland.

You by no means had to be a Harriet Tubman or a Frederick Douglass to
be an Underground Railroad hero. There were many other heroes whose
stories are still coming to light. Those chosen for this book as heroes of the
Underground Railroad in the Washington, D.C. region are not famous, but
they should be for their qualities and the examples they set.

The Underground Railroad in D.C. is still largely unknown to the public,
despite Stanley Harrold's excellent articles and monograph *Subversives:*

Antislavery Community in Washington, D.C., 1828–1865. There are also books focusing on the most famous escape from D.C. on the ship the *Pearl* (Mary Kay Ricks's *Escape on the Pearl* and Josephine Pacheco's *The Pearl*), on freedom seeker Senator Blanche Bruce (Lawrence Otis Graham's *The Senator and the Socialite*) and freedmen's aid worker Elizabeth Keckley (Jennifer Fleischer's *Mrs. Lincoln and Mrs. Keckly* and Keckley's own memoir, *Behind the Scenes*).

This book is an introduction for those unfamiliar with the area's Underground Railroad history, and for those not yet intrigued by stories based on credible historical evidence. The book draws on research brought to my attention while I worked for seventeen years for the National Park Service's National Underground Railroad Network to Freedom program. I want to share with a wider public the stories I told when invited to speak. Books on most of the people in these pages—the Coopers, the Plummers, the Gants, Leonard Grimes and John Dean—remain to be written.

Among the "heroes," I include accomplices as well as those escaping, whom I call "freedom seekers." I avoid calling the latter "fugitives," because they did not consider that they had broken any law, or "slaves," because their condition was imposed upon them but did not define them. I avoid whenever possible the railroad metaphor that turns those escaping into "passengers" or "packages" and focuses the spotlight only on the "conductors" assisting them.

In this book, the term *Underground Railroad* has a broader meaning (see Background), and its heroes are a broader group than those involved in antebellum orchestrated escapes of enslaved African Americans. Some of the enslaved took it upon themselves to escape with no foreseen help. The trip between slavery and freedom sometimes ended back in slavery. For this reason, I even include someone in the process of buying his freedom who was betrayed and sold south into lifetime enslavement. When some help was offered, it could be more than food and clothing, transportation or shelter—one hero was a lawyer defending freedom seekers in court.

In choosing subjects for the book's chapters, I have sought diversity wherever possible. Regardless of where they ended up, I have chosen individuals from Washington itself and from many surrounding counties—in Maryland, Prince George's and Montgomery Counties; and in Virginia, Fairfax, Prince William and Loudoun Counties. I have included both men and women, freedom seekers and helpers, African Americans and whites, and free and unfree. In some cases, I have focused only on the Underground Railroad incident and its origins, but in others, I have sought to elucidate what impact the heroic actions had on the subsequent life of the hero. I have included women wherever possible, because it is commonly thought that freedom seekers were overwhelmingly men. I have also included women with children to show the special dilemmas they faced.

I call my chapters "stories," but they are based on primary sources from the period, preferably letters, newspaper articles or diaries by those involved as participants or witnesses. It is lucky for the historian that escapes and trials of alleged Underground Railroad operatives were newsworthy, described in newspaper articles or in letters. As evidence-based accounts, parts of the stories are missing, and I have had to be content.

The individuals whose historical profiles are included in this book were chosen as relatively unknown yet well researched by either academic or local historians. Without these historians, I could not have written this book. I have aimed to highlight their meticulous work for a wider public in hopes of exciting interest in some unsung heroes of the Underground Railroad. The chapters are not all parallel snapshots, because research is ongoing.

All illustrations are as directly as possible associated with the stories themselves, and by no means should they limit the imaginations of the readers. For the Underground Railroad, location is crucial—whether at the beginning of the journey in Washington and surrounding counties or at journey's end in Boston or Nantucket. Location, as well as time period, affected the nature of slavery, the possibilities for action and the obstacles to escape. Physical conditions may have changed drastically, however. Each story is still associated with a physical place in the D.C. metropolitan area, whether or not that place is obvious today. Instead of being tied to a building with historic integrity and representative of the relevant period, sites of some of these stories may consist of a sign or a marker by a river, next to a parking lot or on a highway. These places range from the front of the White House, world-famous but not famous for its connection to Ann Maria Weems, to a slave trader's house, now an anonymous private home not open to the public. It is possible to visit parks like Riversdale, plaques like the one on Leonard Grimes's D.C. property or a Montgomery County wayside marker where pursuers apprehended William Chaplin's carriage carrying Garland H. White.

An aim of this book is to dispel stereotypes and misconceptions about the Underground Railroad. A focus on African American agency in the definition extends the time period of the "Underground Railroad" from slavery's beginning in America to the ratification of the Thirteenth Amendment in 1865. Freedom seekers existed before the organized movement in D.C. of

Torrey, Smallwood, Chaplin and Bigelow. Freedom seekers continued to flee until the end of the Civil War.

While working for the National Park Service, I often told the stories in this book to audiences who were fascinated by the resourcefulness, initiative and pluck of those seeking freedom in the Washington area. They found these stories based on historical evidence inspiring and as enthralling as the myths. It is my hope that this book will pique its readers' interest and create a growing demand for stories of freedom seekers and those who helped them in their pursuit of freedom.

I hope to see further documentation of Underground Railroad history and to see local history connect with broader regional stories of the Underground Railroad. In turn, such connections would coordinate and stimulate further research on the Underground Railroad in the Washington area. If this book succeeds in these aims, it will have been worth the effort.

Jenny Masur
Washington, D.C.
July 1, 2018

ACKNOWLEDGEMENTS

F irst, I thank The History Press and my editor, Kate Jenkins, who enabled me to tell these stories.

I must acknowledge those who taught me much of what I know about the Underground Railroad: Diane Miller, Vincent DeForrest, Sheri Jackson, Deanda Johnson, Aaron Mahr, Tara Morrison, Barbara Tagger, Guy Washington and James Hill, who worked with me at the National Underground Railroad Network to Freedom, a National Park Service program.

This book is built on the research of many others. I am indebted to those who were generous in sharing their research with me and allowed me to include it in this book. Many thanks to those people who introduced me to the heroes in the chapters: Alcione Amos, Mary Belcher, Tony Cohen and Elisa Carbone, Kathryn Grover, Stanley Harrold, Fran Karttunen and Barbara White, Lee Lawrence, Deborah Lee and Elaine Thompson, Bryan and Shannon Prince, Victoria Robinson and Anita Jackson, Leigh Ryan and the staff at Riversdale, Sandra Schmidt, Bronwen Souders, Don Wilson, Chris Haley and Maya Davis, and the authors of the National Underground Railroad Network to Freedom applications for the National Capital Region. I cannot forget Hilary Russell, who wrote a groundbreaking report on the Underground Railroad in Washington for the National Park Service.

Too numerous to name are the many archivists and librarians at so many libraries, courthouses, historical societies, museums and archives who tracked down details, images and articles. I single out Libby Oldham,

ACKNOWLEDGEMENTS

Nantucket Historical Association; Elaine McRey, Virginia Room, Fairfax Library; Laura Christiansen, Thomas Balch Library; Darlene Hunter, Ruth E. Lloyd Information Center for Genealogy and Local History, Prince William Library System; Robin Spurlino, The Friends of Springton; Victoria Thompson, Fairfax Circuit Court Historic Records Center; George Almeter, Warsaw Historical Society; and Eric Larson, Historic Records, Clerk of the Circuit Court, Loudoun County. They went beyond the call of duty to help me. I thank them all. In the same category, I have to thank Maryland and Virginia state and county employees at archives, museums, parks and tourist offices like Anne Kyle, who was extremely helpful.

I am grateful to friends and family who supported me and read and commented on parts of the manuscript. I cannot thank Stan Harrold enough for his scholarship on the Underground Railroad in Washington and his help by reading the manuscript.

Although I received help checking the facts in several chapters, all errors are my own.

CHRONOLOGY

Boldface entries are persons/events featured in this book.

1831	Nat Turner Rebellion
	Liberator established
1833	American Antislavery Society
1834	British abolished slavery in empire (includes Canada, British Caribbean)
	New York Vigilance Committee
1835	Snow Riot
1836–44	**Gag Rule in Congress**
1838	Frederick Douglass escaped
	Joshua Giddings elected to Congress
1840	**Leonard Grimes arrested and tried**
1841	*Amistad* Supreme Court decision
1842	**John Douglass escaped Mrs. Sprigg's boardinghouse**
	Prigg v. Pennsylvania Supreme Court decision
	George Latimer arrested
1843	**Poor Robert and Scott escaped Sprigg's boardinghouse**
	Thomas Smallwood and Reverend Charles Torrey escaped capture
1845	**Mark Caesar and Bill Wheeler captured and tried**
	Narrative of the Life of Frederick Douglass published
1846	Alexandria retroceded from D.C.
	Nelson Gant tried
	Reverend Charles Torrey martyred
	Mexican War began
1847	*North Star* founded
	National Era began publication
1848	***Pearl* Affair and *National Era* riots**
	John Quincy Adams died
	Henry Wilson kidnapped from Sprigg's boardinghouse
	Thomas Garrett convicted
1849	Harriet Tubman escaped
1850	Compromise of 1850 (Fugitive Slave Act and end of D.C. slave trade)
	William Chaplin arrested and Allen and Garland caught
	Uncle Tom's Cabin published serially in *National Era*
	Rendition of Thomas Sims
	Rendition of Anthony Burns
1851	Christiana Resistance
1854	Kansas-Nebraska Act

1855	**Ann Maria Weems escaped**
1856	Margaret Garner case
	Bleeding Kansas began
1857	Dred Scott Supreme Court decision
1858	**William Boyd caught**
	Oberlin-Wellington rescue
1859	John Brown's Raid
	Abelman v. Booth Supreme Court decision
1860	Abraham Lincoln elected president
	South Carolina seceded
1861	Fort Sumter attacked (April)
	General Benjamin Butler declared refugees as contraband (May)
	Union troops occupied Alexandria, Virginia (May)
	First Confiscation Act (August)
	Hortense Prout captured
	Garland H. White appeared on Canada West Census
1862	D.C. Emancipation Act
	John Dean arrived in D.C.
	Second Confiscation Act
1863	Emancipation Proclamation
	Recruitment and enlistment of U.S. Colored Troops began
	Plummers escaped
	Andrew Hall case
	John Dean died
1864	Fugitive Slave Act repealed
	Maryland Constitution changed to abolish slavery
1865	General Robert E. Lee surrendered at Appomattox, Virginia
1865	Thirteenth Amendment ratified

BACKGROUND

The following letter, written in a half-legible manner, was published by Harriet Beecher Stowe in *The Key to Uncle Tom's Cabin* (1853), a book written to provide the evidence for her best-selling novel:

febuary 18 1850
Mr Begelow dr sor I rit to you to let you no how i am getin a long had times
her I hav not Had one oyr to go out sid of the place sence I hav bin on et i
put my trust in the lord to halp me I long to hear from you all I retten to hear
from yo all Mr Begelow i hop yo will not for me you no et was not my falt
that I am hear I hop you will nam me to Mr Geden Mr chaplen Mr Baly
to healp me out of et I be leve that if Would mak the les move to et that et
cod be Don i long to hear from my famaly how the ar Geten a long you will
ples to rit to me jest to let me no how tha are geten a long you can rit to me
i remain yous yo umbl servent
thomas Ducket

you can ded rec you letters to thomas Ducke in car of Mr sam ul t harisin
lusana nar byagoler of is for god sake let me hear from you all my wife and
children ar not out of my mine day nor night

The letter expresses the misery and yearning of a bondsman sold south from Washington. It was written, as Harriet Beecher Stowe explained, by "a poor, honest, hard-working slaveman by the name of Thomas Ducket" whose wife had been a passenger on the ship the *Pearl* in 1848. Harriet Beecher Stowe skillfully used the heartbreaking letter to make her readers sympathetic to enslaved African Americans.

This letter demonstrates the predicament of someone whose love for his family pulled him into resistance to slavery. In trying to procure freedom, the Ducket family resorted to those involved in the Underground Railroad. The Duckets were caught in the dilemma of either enduring slavery in D.C. or taking a very great risk of punishment, death or sale south. Their crime in the eyes of the white community and the federal government was their acting on their desire

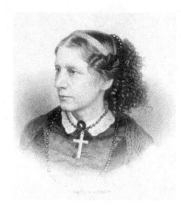

Harriet Beecher Stowe was involved in helping some of the freedom seekers from the failed escape on the ship the *Pearl*. *Library of Congress.*

for control of their own lives and for relief from suffering. Ducket wanted his family out of slavery.

In order to make arrangements for a large escape, operatives of the Underground Railroad had hired a captain and a ship, the *Pearl*, to carry about seventy of those fleeing slavery down the Potomac River, into the Chesapeake Bay and on to points north. Such an escape depended on the cooperation of the African American community with African American and white planners. The authorities supposed Ducket had helped or at least had knowledge of the man or men who planned the *Pearl* escape. In the letter, Ducket named several of those antislavery white men presumably in on the secret plans for the *Pearl*—Jacob Bigelow, William Chaplin, Joshua Giddings and Gamaliel Bailey. Ducket was either working with those masterminding the scheme or those who at least knew of their activities, since the activities were partially on behalf of him and his threatened family. In return for his stubborn silence protecting these men and Underground Railroad operations, Ducket counted on the safety of himself and his family. He was disappointed. His fate lay in lonely sale to Louisiana, a place known to slave dealer and enslaved African American alike as a nightmarish destination. Without news, he was left to imagine dire consequences for his family. Ducket's suffering can be conjured up by reading *Twelve Years a Slave* (1853), an account by Solomon Northup, someone else sold from Washington to Louisiana. It is not known whether Ducket's letter was answered or acted upon.

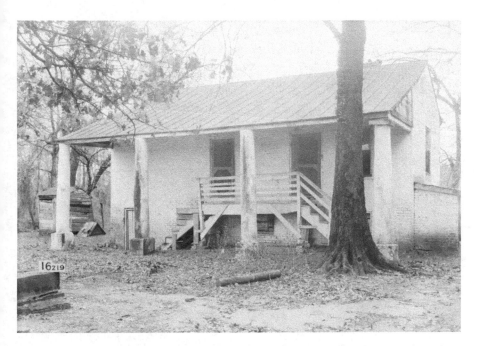

This Louisiana slave quarters may resemble where Thomas Ducket lived. *Historic American Buildings Survey, Library of Congress.*

From the beginning of slavery in America, there was always a small percentage of bondsmen who sought to escape at any cost. There is no known total for freedom seekers, but compared to the total enslaved population (by 1860, almost four million), the number was small. The numbers of freedom seekers were often exaggerated by both pro- and antislavery supporters to boost their very different points of view. The trickle became a flood once the Civil War (1861–65) began and enslaved people realized the Union army would protect them. The surge continued until slavery was legally ended in 1865 with passage of the Thirteenth Amendment. As in the case of the *Pearl* attempt, escapes were not always successful, a factor not necessarily part of the mathematics of estimating the size of the Underground Railroad.

If the Underground Railroad is thought of as "resistance to slavery through flight," that gives the term a broader meaning, a wider geography and a longer time span than restricting it to antebellum organized networks. The broader definition gives agency to the freedom seeker, emphasizing those who took the greatest initiative and greatest risks. Underground Railroad heroes include freedom seekers and the operatives and accomplices

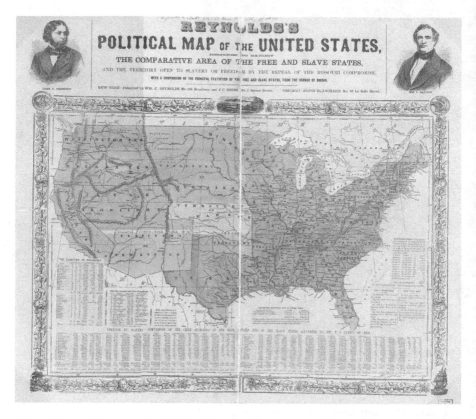

"Reynolds's political map of the United States, designed to exhibit the comparative area of the free and slave states and the territory open to slavery or freedom by the repeal of the Missouri Compromise," 1856. *Library of Congress.*

who helped them. These heroes are both men and women, white and African American, free and enslaved. Flight to freedom can be considered a two-way journey, because some captured freedom seekers were returned to slavery, and some free and almost free African Americans were kidnapped into slavery.

Central to the history of the Underground Railroad are the institution of slavery and the society that not only condoned it but also made it legal. U.S. emancipation started with Vermont (1777). It spread to northern states like Pennsylvania (1780) and Massachusetts (1783), often in a gradual form that delayed freedom until an enslaved person reached a stipulated age. Slavery, however, continued to be legal in the United States until the end of the Civil War, because the slaveholding border states stayed in the Union. Although the North eliminated slavery for life and fought to keep it out of

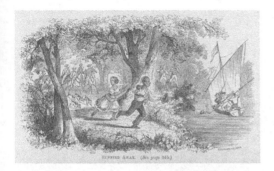

Running Away (1864) summarizes the flight of a family, chased by bloodhounds and slave catchers, on their way to an escape by water. *New York Public Library*.

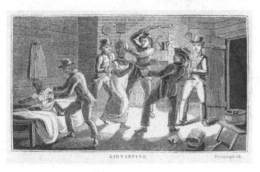

Kidnapping (1822) from Jesse Torrey, *American Slave Trade*, graphically represents a danger for free blacks. *New York Public Library*.

the territories, the invention of the cotton gin (1793) made southern cotton profitable through its sale to Britain and New England. Using enslaved labor, cotton cultivation boomed in the South. Northern banks, insurance companies and factories benefited from slavery.

Those in slavery refused to accept their condition, considering that it did not define them. We will honor them by calling them not "slaves" but "enslaved people" or "bondsmen." Of all involved in resistance to slavery, those called here "freedom seekers" (not the pejorative "runaways" or "fugitives") shouldered the biggest risk in flight—death, punishment or sale. Many showed courage and took any opportunity offered. They were usually the ones to initiate flight, and they had the most to lose. Fleeing slavery was considered a crime. Still, they wanted freedom so much that they were often willing to try escape several times. They did not wait for help from strangers, although they took it with caution. When necessary and feasible, those escaping offered resistance when stopped by slave catchers or offered local help, as at Christiana, Pennsylvania (1851). If lucky, they escaped captors and reached a place of permanent refuge that had abolished slavery, like Mexico (1829) or the British Empire—especially Canada and the British Caribbean (1834). If unlucky, their attempts ended in jail, then in court and then a return to slavery. A wartime ploy was for men to join the military

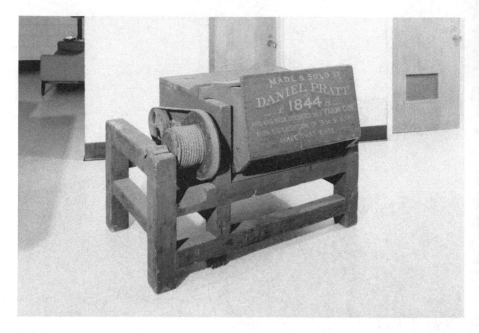

The invention of the cotton gin revolutionized the cultivation of cotton, which turned into a cash crop dependent on a strong domestic slave trade. *Library of Congress.*

forces during the American Revolution, War of 1812 and Civil War in return for a promise of freedom.

Accomplices came from all backgrounds and could act once or repeatedly. Not all were part of or set up networks of help and refuge for freedom seekers. If some of the accomplices intended to be martyrs or heroes, others only reacted when they were suddenly faced with a freedom seeker. Some will remain nameless or unknown as supporters of fleeing bondsmen.

More than half the modern states in the country have an association with Underground Railroad history, as either starting points, parts of routes, destinations or illegal refuges of freedom seekers. It may come as a surprise to learn that Washington, D.C., a southern city and the U.S. capital, was a destination, a stop and a hub for the Underground Railroad in the eighteenth and nineteenth centuries. Over two centuries, runaway advertisements from the Washington, D.C. area and letters and diaries of slave owners from Alexandria, Georgetown and outlying areas testify to flight and attempts at capture.

From D.C.'s beginnings, the sight of slavery was everywhere—in the streets, markets and shops; in homes, hotels and taverns. Bondsmen built the White House and the Capitol and were part of the workforce digging

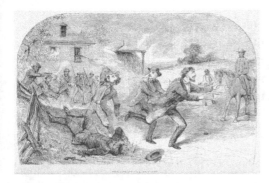

Left: "Christiana Tragedy." The incident in 1851 demonstrated the ability of a supportive community to resist slave catchers. *New York Public Library*.

Below: E. Sachse & Co. published this "View of Washington City, D.C." in 1862. *Library of Congress*.

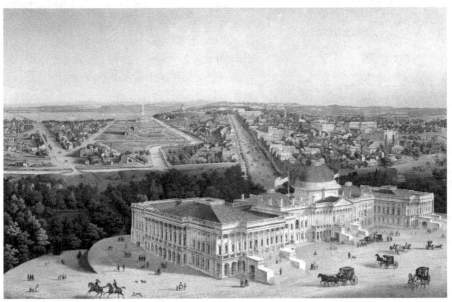

the Chesapeake & Ohio Canal for the first couple of years. Visitors arriving for the first time to Washington were shocked by the coffles, whippings and public auctions of people of color. They discovered that Congress, which had jurisdiction over the District and was dominated by southerners, was not about to abolish slavery or the slave trade in the capital city. Congress was not ready to ban the convenient use of enslaved labor on construction of public buildings.

Washington had become the seat of the federal government in 1800 after being created as a ten-mile square formed from two slave states, Maryland and Virginia. The newly created District followed the laws of the states from which it was formed until Congress enacted the District's own laws. Slavery was legal. In the beginning, parts of the District were little developed;

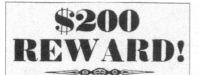

$200 REWARD!

Ran away from his owner [a Lady residing near Upper Marlboro, Prince George's County, Md.] on or about the 12th inst. of this month, a bright Mulatto man named Frank, a carpenter by trade, he is about five feet 9 or 10 inches high, light grey eyes, slow in speech, and very good personal appearance, about twenty-five years of age, his clothing good.

One Hundred dollars will be paid if apprehended within thirty miles of home, if more than thirty, the above reward, provided he be secured in Jail so that his owner gets him again.

W. D. BOWIE,

for the owner,

Buena Vista Post Office, Prince George's Co. Md. February 14th, 1853.

Such a runaway ad was typical of Prince George's County, Maryland. *New York Public Library.*

Georgetown and Alexandria were the urban areas, and the District depended on its neighbors in Maryland and Virginia for manpower and agricultural products. In terms of slavery, there were no boundaries between the District and surrounding counties where slavery was entrenched— Prince William, Fairfax and Loudoun in Virginia, and Montgomery and Prince George's in Maryland. Throughout this region, slave owners would move bondsmen from one residence to another and one job to another without consideration of borders as they inherited, moved, married, bought new real estate and hired out unneeded bondsmen. Escape routes connected various parts of the region.

While still intermeshed with slavery in surrounding areas, after 1800, Washington became differentiated from surrounding counties by its growing number of free African Americans and its role as a labor market for hired-out bondsmen. That gave D.C.'s free African Americans critical mass to create community organizations like independent churches, schools and a mutual aid society. Table 1 compares the percentages of those enslaved in nearby jurisdictions and shows the rapid increase in free African Americans in D.C. The whites were right to worry about their help to escaping bondsmen. Free African Americans had a strong motivation to aid escapes, although they were at risk of legal punishment. It was unlikely that there was any free African American who did not have a friend or relative who was enslaved. Free men knew they could be kidnapped by slave traders or picked up by the local slave catcher as a "runaway."

Because of its growing free population, Washington was a magnet for bondsmen from surrounding counties looking for refuge from slavery by switching names, forging papers or changing their appearances. Washington could be a final or only an intermediate stop. Within the region, counties were united by potential routes to freedom that crisscrossed it. Main roads like the Rockville Pike, Montgomery Road and Leesburg Pike went to Washington. For help or advice while planning flight, African Americans had networks of family and friends across the region with whom they kept in

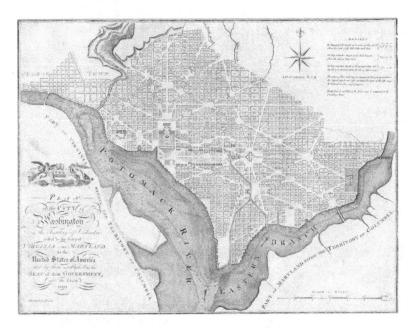

"Plan of the City of Washington in the Territory of Columbia" is dated 1800. *Library of Congress.*

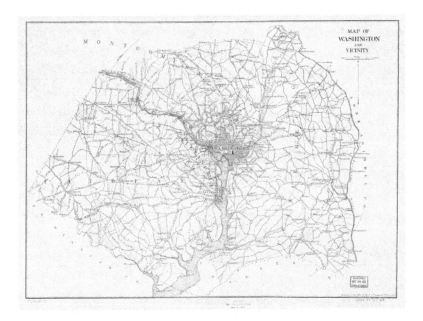

"Map of Washington and Vicinity," U.S. Geological Survey, 1882, shows Fairfax County and Alexandria to the west of D.C., Montgomery County to the north and Prince George's County to the east. *Library of Congress.*

ENSLAVED PEOPLE BY JURISDICTION, 1800–1860

COUNTY	1800	1810	1820	1830	1840	1850	1860
DC*							
Total**	14,093	24,023	33,039	39,834	43,711	51,687	75,080
Enslaved	3,244	5,395	6,377	6,119	4,694	3,687	3,185
Free	783	2,549	4,048	6,152	8,360	10,059	11,131
%Enslaved	5.5	22.4	19.3	15.4	10.7	7.1	4.2
Fairfax							
Total							
Enslaved	13,317	13,111	11,404	9,204	9,370	10,682	11,834
Free	6,078	5,492	4,673	4,001	3,453	3,250	3,116
%Enslaved	45.6	41.9	40.9	43.5	36.9	30.4	26.3
Prince William							
Total							
Enslaved	12,733	11,311	9,419	9,330	8,144	8,129	8,565
Free	5,416	5,220	4,380	3,842	2,767	2,498	2,356
%Enslaved	42.5	46.1	46.5	41.2	34.0	30.7	27.5
Loudoun							
Total							
Enslaved	20,523	21,338	22,702	21,939	20,431	22,079	21,774
Free	4,990	5,147	5,729	5,363	5,273	5,641	5,501
%Enslaved	24.3	24.1	25.2	24.4	25.8	25.5	25.3
Montgomery							
Total			16,400	19,816	14,669	15,860	18,322
Enslaved	6,288	7,572	6,396	6,447	5,135	5,114	5,421
Free	8,770	10,408	922	1,266	1,313	1,311	1,552
%Enslaved			39.0	32.5	35.0	32.2	29.6
Prince George's							
Total			20,216	20,474	19,539	21,549	23,327
Enslaved	12,191	9,189	11,185	11,585	10,636	11,510	12,479
Free	8,994	11,400	1,096	1,202	1,080	1,138	1,198
%Enslaved			55.3	56.6	54.4	53.4	53.5

*Without Alexandria
**Total population of whites and African Americans
Sources: Marylanders [census year]: African American Population by County, Status & Gender,
http://www.slavery.msa.maryland/html/research/census; Racial Composition of the Population of the
District of Columbia 1800–2010, http://www.matthewbgilmore.word.press.com/district-of-columbia-
population-history; Population of Virginia [census year]; http://www.virginiaplaces.org/population/
pop[census year]numbers.html.

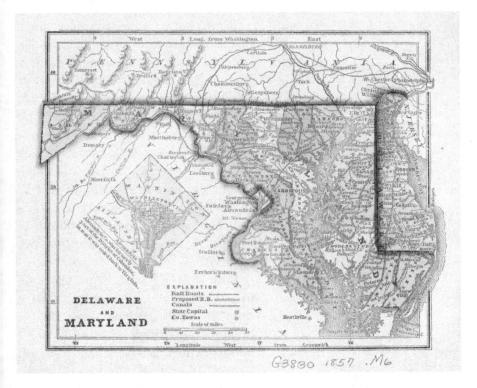

G3830 1857 .M6

Above: Delaware and Maryland nestle the Chesapeake Bay in a Morse & Gaston map, 1857. *Library of Congress.*

Opposite: This chart is a comparison of enslaved populations, 1800–1860, by Washington-area jurisdictions.

touch through visits, mingling in markets, stints as "hired out" workers in D.C., even at times through letters.

Washington's location was fateful for its association with the Underground Railroad. Washington is situated on the Potomac River, which divides Maryland and Virginia and feeds into the Chesapeake Bay. The river and the Chesapeake & Ohio Canal were paths to follow northward. Ships headed out of the D.C. area as far as Boston or Britain—ships on which freedom seekers could stow away or work as sailors. The District is not located far from the Mason-Dixon line, which, already drawn in the 1760s, became accepted as the boundary between North and South. The closest northern state to D.C. is Pennsylvania, long associated with the Quakers' antislavery stance.

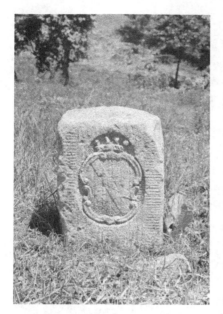

This Mason-Dixon line marker is in Zora, Adams County, Pennsylvania. As northern states abolished slavery, the Mason-Dixon line became the boundary between slavery and freedom. *Historic American Buildings Survey, Library of Congress.*

Resistance to slavery through flight in the D.C. area deserves examination because of the special status of the U.S. capital. Washington was a federal entity like the territories, so Congress could change the status of slavery and the slave trade there. Escapes from Washington or surrounding areas could in turn impact Congress, creating further discussion of the legality and morality of slavery. In Washington, local history often gets overshadowed by national history. In the case of resistance to slavery, the two converge.

With the end of U.S. participation in the legal international slave trade in 1808, traders turned to the domestic slave trade and the lucrative opportunities in Maryland and Virginia. Patterns of enslaved labor had changed with the switch from tobacco to grains and livestock, creating surplus workers. The problem of the excess labor force in Maryland and Virginia was solved too often by feeding the voracious slave trade to the Lower South rather than by manumission or self-purchase. As a result, the enslaved population was well aware of the growing likelihood of separation from loved ones by sale. They feared the brutal working conditions in the Lower South. That alone spurred escapes.

During the first half of the nineteenth century, the growing antislavery movement focused on D.C. as a symbol of the shocking state of a republic based on slavery and slavery's supporters. Slaveholders felt pride in slavery in the nation's capital, which seemed to legitimize the institution. Visiting abolitionists and local Quakers paid special attention to the slave traders in D.C. Northern antislavery advocates became determined to end the slave trade and slavery in D.C., writing poems, primers, almanacs and newspaper articles promoting their cause. Already by the 1820s, antislavery materials circulated in D.C.

Two influential national abolitionist newspapers spread abolitionists' words. William Lloyd Garrison founded the *Liberator* in Boston (1831); the

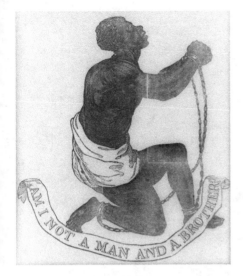

Left: The "Am I not a man and a brother?" figure on this broadside was an abolitionist emblem of the American Anti-Slavery Society. *Library of Congress.*

Below: *United States Slave Trade* (1830). The Capitol stands in the background of this print, clearly referring to the slave trade in D.C. *Library of Congress.*

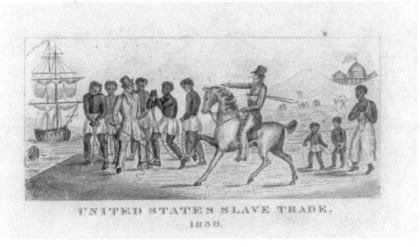

North Star in Rochester was founded by Frederick Douglass (1847). Both were read not only by white northerners but also by free African Americans and bondsmen in the North and South whenever they could obtain them. Washington had its own antislavery newspaper as of 1847, the *National Era*. It was edited judiciously by Gamaliel Bailey, a moderate whose aim was to create a quality periodical appealing to the as yet unconvinced.

Any attempt at escape from slavery in D.C. was publicized as well in a variety of local newspapers, applauded by the abolitionist minority and decried by the adherents of slavery who dominated the city. Any incident that occurred in D.C, whether violent or nonviolent, could become fodder

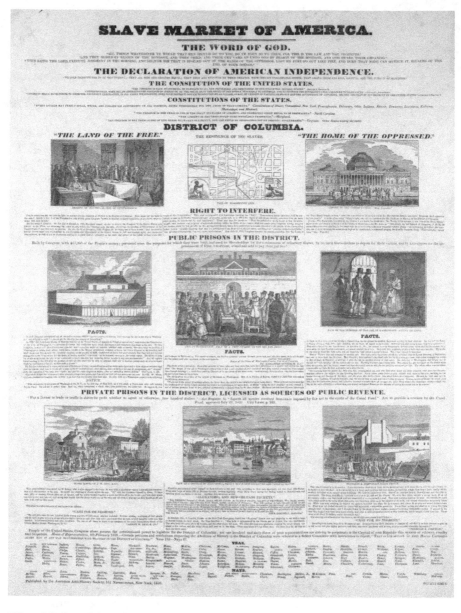

"Slave Market of America," an 1836 broadside, was published by the American Anti-Slavery Society as part of a campaign against slavery in Washington. *Library of Congress.*

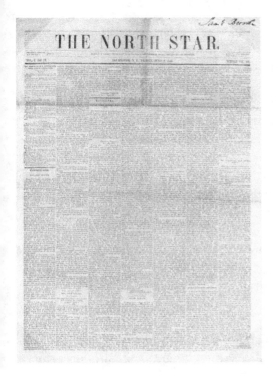

The *North Star* was to be a beacon of
liberty. *Library of Congress.*

for both the abolitionist press and the proslavery press. A riot or resistance
during a bondsman's recapture could be bandied about in Congress and
frighten not only D.C.'s inhabitants but also congressmen residing seasonally
in D.C. and slaveholders in Maryland and Virginia.

Antislavery societies had formed across the nation from the 1770s on.
By the 1830s, the societies, especially northern women's societies, were
flooding their representatives in Congress with petitions to end slavery
and the slave trade in D.C. They made D.C. a target because action by
Congress would not interfere with states' rights. To restrict discussion of
antislavery petitions and of slavery, southern Congressmen voted into place
a Gag Rule starting in 1836. After his presidency, John Quincy Adams was
elected to Congress, where he served from 1831 to 1848. Adams and his
antislavery allies targeted the ongoing Gag Rule (1836–44).

The Supreme Court heard cases like *United States v. Schooner Amistad*
(Amistad, 1841), *Scott v. Sanford* (Dred Scott, 1857) and *Abelman v. Booth*
(1859), all crucial decisions for abolitionists and African Americans. Cases
in Washington's courts established local freedom of speech for abolitionists,
challenged Congress's Fugitive Slave Acts (1793, 1850) or tested compensated
emancipation.

Because of debates in Congress and other events, D.C. was a tense city. After two revolts by enslaved African Americans in Virginia—Gabriel's Conspiracy (1800) and Nat Turner's Rebellion (1831)—the white community was uneasy. It took only an excuse linked to abolitionists for riots to erupt in Washington. Such riots threatened the African American community's status quo, legally and/or physically.

The Snow Riot (1835) occurred as a result of two events blamed on the corrupting influence of abolitionists. Arthur Bowen and Reuben Crandall triggered the riot. Bondsman Arthur Bowen tried to kill his owner, the widow of the U.S. Capitol architect Dr. William Thornton. Within a few days, a newcomer, white northern abolitionist Reuben Crandall, was found with incriminating materials wrapped around his botanical specimens for teaching. Worse, he confessed to supporting immediate emancipation. Bowen and Crandall were almost lynched before mobs were contained and the two men were safely jailed. Because of a rumored insult by African American Beverly Snow, the mob channeled its anti-abolitionist rage on Snow's restaurant and on African American schools, churches and homes. As a result, African American leaders either stayed out of sight or fled the city. Worried by the two incidents, the city government placed more restrictions on free African Americans.

In 1848, more than seventy freedom seekers from the region tried to escape down the Potomac River on the ship the *Pearl* and failed. A Washington mob placed blame for the planning of the escape on antislavery proponents, in particular on Gamaliel Bailey, publisher of the *National Era*. During several days of riots, the editor and his press were saved from the mob only by the intervention of the mayor and prominent citizens.

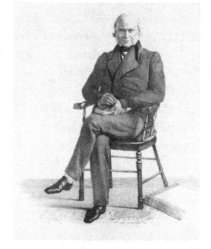

The attempted escape inspired Harriet Beecher Stowe to write her provocative best seller *Uncle Tom's Cabin* in 1850, first published serially by the *National Era*. The most important impact of the *Pearl* for African Americans in Washington was the impetus it gave to the Compromise of 1850, passed after much negotiation in Congress. Its provisions had both a

John Quincy Adams became an antislavery voice in Congress after he retired from the presidency. *Library of Congress.*

40

positive and negative effect on African Americans in D.C. On the one hand, among other measures, the compromise abolished the slave trade in D.C., a symbolic act as the trade promptly moved to Alexandria, no longer part of D.C. On the other, it established the Fugitive Slave Act of 1850.

More punitive than the 1793 Fugitive Slave Act, the 1850 act threatened accomplices of freedom seekers with heavy fines and required all citizens to cooperate in the capture of "fugitives." The act eroded even minimal rights for those bondsmen caught and accused of breaking the law and denied them due process. The act placed the burden of enforcement on the federal government. The act set up a system of federal commissioners to hear cases of captured freedom seekers, but bondsmen could not testify. Only white witnesses were needed to establish the owner's claim. The system made it more lucrative for commissioners to rule a person a "slave" than not, thus weighing the commissioners' decisions in that direction.

Horrid Massacre in Virginia (1831) shows the shock and horror felt after Nat Turner's Rebellion. *Library of Congress.*

In reaction to the Fugitive Slave Acts, northern states developed two series of "personal liberty laws." The laws were designed to protect freedom seekers on northern soil from a return to slavery by replacing federal responsibility to capture freedom seekers with state laws on the matter. In the 1820s, for example, Pennsylvania and New York enacted laws to prevent kidnapping of free African Americans and to protect those suspected of being freedom seekers. In *Prigg v. Pennsylvania* (1842), the U.S. Supreme Court struck down the first set of such laws by overruling Pennsylvania's law of 1827. The decision triggered the second round of personal liberty laws beginning in the 1840s, such as those of Massachusetts and Pennsylvania. State jails and officials were not to be used to capture and return "fugitives." In 1859, the Supreme Court decision *Abelman v. Booth* ruled ten states' personal liberty laws unconstitutional, although Wisconsin refused to abide by the ruling.

The 1850 Fugitive Slave Act caused many desperate freedom seekers settled in the northern U.S. to flee to Canada. It emboldened activists and inspired a number of rescues stretching through the 1850s, of which the most famous was the Oberlin-Wellington Rescue in Ohio (1858). John Brown's Raid on the Harpers Ferry arsenal in order to arm bondsmen for a rebellion (1859) escalated sectional divisions. It strengthened northern negative opinions of slavery and southern fears of violence.

In D.C. by the 1840s and 1850s, antislavery feeling was sufficiently strong and the African American community sufficiently desperate to support the organization of a formal escape and financial network, in addition to individual escapes and accomplices who worked on their own. The 1850 Fugitive Slave Act was a final motivation. Antislavery activists, mostly northerners, formed a small community in D.C. Members chose different strategies to help freedom seekers—raising money for self-purchase, facilitating manumission,

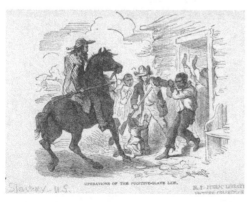

Operations of the Fugitive Slave Law provides an abolitionist perspective on the results of the law. *New York Public Library.*

guiding court proceedings, speechifying in Congress and aiding escape. Cooperation created an organized Underground Railroad as white activists allied themselves with members of the local African American community and with a network of white and African American sympathizers to the north. From the 1840s through the 1850s, in one form or another, there were successive biracial networks organized by Reverend Charles Torrey and Thomas Smallwood; William Chaplin; and Jacob Bigelow.

When Reverend Charles Torrey died of tuberculosis in the Maryland penitentiary at age thirty-three in 1846, Massachusetts abolitionists made a martyr of him for his work on the Underground Railroad. They buried him with great honors and a monument in Cambridge, Massachusetts. From 1841 to 1843, Reverend Torrey had teamed up with Thomas Smallwood, a freed African American from Prince George's County. Jailing in Maryland had earlier confronted Torrey with the suffering of an enslaved family and convinced him of the need to take on the slavery establishment. Smallwood and Torrey worked together with help from the black and white communities as the two organized, financed and implemented an escape route north using ever-changing meeting places for guides and freedom seekers and arranging refuges along the way. In 1843, the D.C. Auxiliary Guard captured a contingent of freedom seekers where Torrey and Smallwood kept the horses and wagon for transport. Smallwood and his partner escaped, but John Bush, an African American associate, was arrested. Torrey continued his provocative rescues. After tangling with the powerful Baltimore slave dealer Hope Slatter, who made sure he was arrested, Reverend Torrey was tried and sentenced to serve for six years in the prison where he died. Bush was eventually acquitted. Smallwood and his family escaped to Canada, where Smallwood wrote his autobiography (1851) with details of the joint Underground Railroad operations.

After Reverend Torrey's death, his admirer William Chaplin came to D.C. from New York and took over management of the Underground Railroad network. At first, he tried to help the enslaved African Americans with whom he became acquainted by fundraising for redemption from slavery and by arranging legal help. Eventually, he saw no substitute for enabling escape, so he used his biracial Underground Railroad contacts, which by this time extended to include New York philanthropists and activists.

Chaplin twice provoked national headlines. The first time was indirectly, because of his concealed involvement in 1848's *Pearl* Affair. Chaplin had been pulled into planning the *Pearl's* journey. The organizers managed to escape unmasking. The burden of capture fell onto most of the passengers,

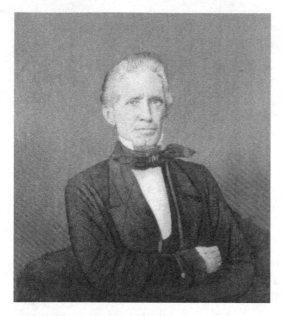

Daniel Drayton, captain on the *Pearl*, suffered imprisonment until pardoned. *Library of Congress.*

who were sold south, and the two captains, who were convicted in 1848 and imprisoned until pardoned by President Millard Fillmore in 1852. One of the captains, Daniel Drayton, never recovered and committed suicide in 1857.

The second time was just before passage of the 1850 Fugitive Slave Act, when a posse caught Chaplin with two freedom seekers. A shoot-out ensued. Levels of anxiety rose in Washington. Chaplin was jailed and went to trial in both Washington and Rockville, Maryland. Much praised and reviled, Chaplin feared a death like Reverend Torrey's. Freed on bail, he fled to New York State, where he spread the news of his exploits on the lecture circuit.

A colleague of Chaplin's, a lawyer named Jacob Bigelow, took over Underground Railroad operations. Cooperating with vigilance committees in New York and Philadelphia, he kept a lower profile than Chaplin or Torrey, even when involved in the applauded escape of Ann Maria Weems. He was not discouraged by or perhaps was even further motivated by the 1850 Fugitive Slave Act and the 1857 Dred Scott decision declaring the impossibility of an African American ever becoming a citizen. Bigelow continued to lead the Underground Railroad until 1858, when he withdrew from his role because of a questionable handling of funds.

Meanwhile, the tension building between North and South over slavery in the territories led to the Kansas-Nebraska Act (1854), which undid the balancing act created by the Missouri Compromise (1820). That in turn

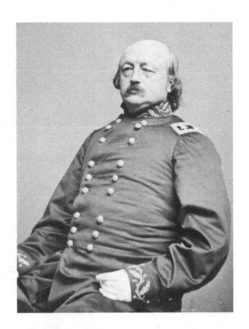

Major General Benjamin F. Butler, previously a lawyer and politician, was the Union general commanding Fort Monroe when bondsmen arrived seeking refuge in 1861. *Library of Congress.*

led to formation of the Republican Party and Bleeding Kansas (1856–59). Abraham Lincoln was elected president in 1860, and southern states began to secede. The Civil War began with the attack on Fort Sumter in April 1861.

The war was about slavery, but loyal states like Maryland and Delaware were allowed to maintain slavery to keep them in the Union. In May 1861, General Benjamin Butler used a legal stratagem at Fort Monroe, near Norfolk, Virginia. He declared fleeing bondsmen to be contraband of war under the law because they were enemy "property" used for the Confederate effort. When Congress passed the D.C. Emancipation Act in April 1862, all enslaved persons in D.C. were freed and owners loyal to the Union compensated.

As an island of freedom in a slaveholding region, D.C. attracted Maryland and Virginia refugees from slavery. Army protection and jobs were an added incentive to flee to Washington. Population ballooned. These refugees were called "contrabands" because of General Butler's decision. They had an ambiguous status, neither legally free nor enslaved. Many were destitute, in need of housing, clothing and guidance. The government placed those who could not find their own housing in "contraband camps" beginning at Duff's Green, then Camp Barker, then Mason's Island and then Freedman's Village. These refugees tended to be elderly, sick and women with children. Able-bodied men and women sought jobs. When the Emancipation Proclamation

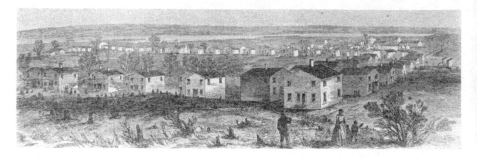

Freedman's Village was a model settlement for "contrabands." *Library of Congress.*

(1863) opened the door to African American enlistment, almost 200,000 African Americans eventually joined Union military forces. In D.C., many male refugees took the promise of freedom and joined up, leaving their families behind in D.C. to manage as they could while the soldiers waited for months to be paid.

Some among the established free African American community and among the abolitionists reached out to help these refugees. For example, D.C.-based African American dressmaker and designer Elizabeth Keckley raised money for the refugees while traveling with Mary Todd Lincoln and through founding the Contraband Relief Association. Harriet Jacobs and her daughter came to Alexandria to be teachers and freedmen's aid workers providing for the sick and needy. Several white abolitionists in D.C. founded the National Freedman's Relief Association of D.C. All over the North, churches and antislavery societies collected clothes and other necessities for refugees. Both black and white teachers went south to staff new black schools.

During the Civil War, the Fugitive Slave Act remained in effect and was enforced on freedom seekers from Maryland, where slavery was still legal. Abolitionist lawyers like John Dean who were D.C. outsiders tested the legitimacy of the act for the territories and D.C. by defending those bondsmen caught in the District. The repeal of the Fugitive Slave Act in June 1864 was an important milestone toward the end of federal support for slavery. The need for the Underground Railroad ended with the passage of the Thirteenth Amendment, which legally freed all bondsmen.

PART I

ESCAPING FROM SLAVERY

1

MARY AND ARTHUR COOPER

From Fairfax County to Nantucket

T he story of the Cooper family rescue in Nantucket can be pieced together from several sources. Camillus Griffith and Thomas Mackril Macy provided sworn testimony in court in Boston. Anna Gardner and William Mitchell wrote down their memories. There were several New Bedford and Nantucket newspaper accounts starting in 1822 and continuing through the 1870s, while those with immediate knowledge of the incident were still alive.

The grapevine spread the rumor of slave catchers on Nantucket. Before dawn on October 24, 1822, a protective crowd of African American men, women and children gathered around Mary and Arthur Cooper's house on Angola Street near Nantucket's African American neighborhood of New Guinea. Word quickly spread to the white community through the efforts of a worried African American cowherd named George Washington. Key white men from nearby Vestal Street mobilized to foil the slave catchers, anxious to help their neighbors and maintain Nantucket's fame as a refuge for freedom seekers.

Washington rushed to the house of Quaker William Mitchell to enlist help against the threat to the Cooper family's continued life in freedom. Mitchell sent Washington on to Gilbert Coffin, who in turn sent word to Sylvanus Macy, an enterprising man whose career would encompass cod fishing and whale hunting, shoemaking and manufacturing spermaceti candles. Mitchell sent someone else to the Quaker abolitionist Oliver Gardner, whom Mitchell would later remember as the "great engineer" of the rescue plan. In the

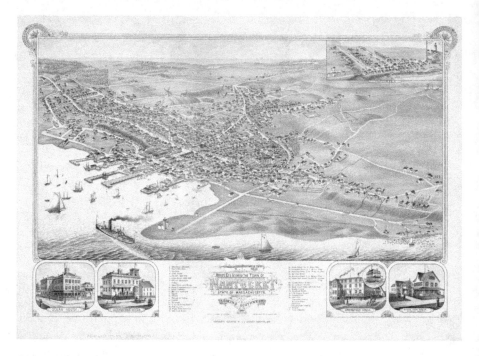

Bird's-eye view of the town of Nantucket in the State of Massachusetts: looking southwest: 1881, is a lithograph by Beck and Paul. *Norman B. Leventhal Map Collection, Boston Public Library.*

1860s, Mitchell claimed that the slave catchers were armed and that the "skill" of Oliver Gardner and the reasoning of Gilbert and Sylvanus averted a massacre.

The crowd around the house before dawn was far from friendly to the four "gentlemanly" callers who were at the Coopers' front door. The crowd was angry. One caller identified himself as Camillus Griffith, a slaveholder from Virginia who was an agent for another slave owner in Virginia. By his side were two Boston deputy marshals who were accompanying him to make official the arrest of Arthur Cooper and his family under the 1793 Fugitive Slave Act. When Griffith addressed himself to the man he guessed to be the crowd's leader, a white Nantucket Quaker named Francis G. Macy, Macy delayed him by making inquiries into his credentials and the authority of his papers. Macy and his fellow Quakers forced Griffith to read aloud the warrant for arrest of the Coopers and the power of attorney from Alexandria lawyer David Ricketts, who claimed ownership of the Coopers.

Delaying tactics continued. Francis Macy's son Sylvanus declared the papers a forgery and harangued the agent and constables with indignant words. Griffith would remember when later testifying in Boston that he was told emphatically that Nantucket was not the South. The Macys in no uncertain words stated that Massachusetts did not recognize slavery and did not want any escaped bondsmen returned to slavery. Instead, Massachusetts residents welcomed African Americans to come to man their whaling ships. When Alfred Folger, the local magistrate, arrived, he backed up the Coopers' defenders, warning Griffith that if he tried to bother the freedom seekers, the magistrate would arrest him and put him in jail or send him back to the judge in Boston. When Griffith referred to the overarching power of federal law, the magistrate did not accept the argument that Massachusetts laws were inferior to those of the federal government. (In fact, it was not until 1823, a year after the rescue of the Coopers, that Massachusetts chief justice Isaac Parker ruled that the 1793 Fugitive Slave Act overrode Massachusetts laws in *Commonwealth of Massachusetts v. Camillus Griffith*.)

Meanwhile, the mood of the crowd continued to be ominous. Deputy Marshal Taylor and other men were assigned to guard against escape from the back of the house. The crowd's taunts frightened them to such an extent

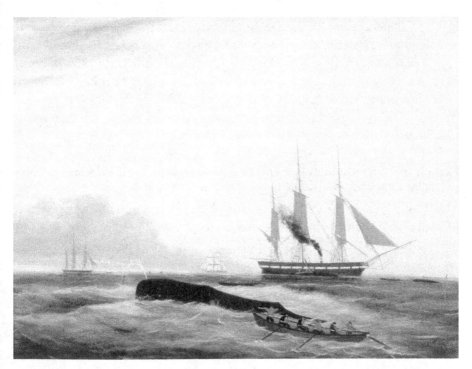

The whaling ship *Islander* was painted about 1860 by an unknown artist. *Courtesy of Nantucket Historical Association.*

that they left their post and returned to the front of the house. The Coopers took advantage of this lack of surveillance to flee, according to Griffith, through a window. Arthur disguised himself in a Quaker broad-brimmed hat and coat borrowed from, respectively, Oliver Gardner and his brother-in-law Thomas Mackril Macy, who had maneuvered themselves to the back of the house. Quakers whisked the Coopers away to a hiding place at Oliver and Hannah Macy Gardner's home. According to Mitchell's story, Oliver and several of his party took Mary and the children on their shoulders and climbed fences to carry them to safety. By the time Griffith gained entrance to the Coopers' house, he was chagrined to find it empty.

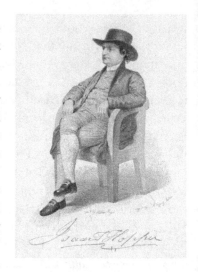

Quaker Isaac Hopper is dressed in typical "plain" dress. *New York Public Library*.

The Coopers stayed in the Gardner house until the slave owner's agent and the marshal left the island. The escape was a coup, as the Cooper family consisted not just of the adults Mary and Arthur, but also their four children, Eliza Ann, Cyrus, Randolph and Robert, all of whom had been born by 1822, according to the King (Cooper family) Bible. In fact, at the time of the escape, Mary was nine months pregnant. Arthur Cooper Jr. was born on October 29, 1822, while the family was in hiding.

Griffith and the constables sailed back to nearby New Bedford. There, Griffith tried to seize John Randolph, who had come from Virginia with the Coopers, but thanks to local Quakers Thomas Rotch (cousin of Francis G. Macy) and William Swain, Griffith was placed in prison. He was convicted of assault and battery and false imprisonment of Randolph. He was not himself released from jail until after Randolph's escape to Barbados by way of New York. A mysterious free "colored" man named William Butler was said to have helped and accompanied the Coopers and Randolph on the freedom seekers' escape vessel. However, the authorities were unable to find him and to extradite him from Massachusetts as requested by the acting Virginia governor.

In 1817 or 1818, along with John Randolph ("Randolph"), Arthur Cooper (then "George") and his family had sailed on the *Regulator* from Alexandria, Virginia, a city across the Potomac River from Georgetown and at that time

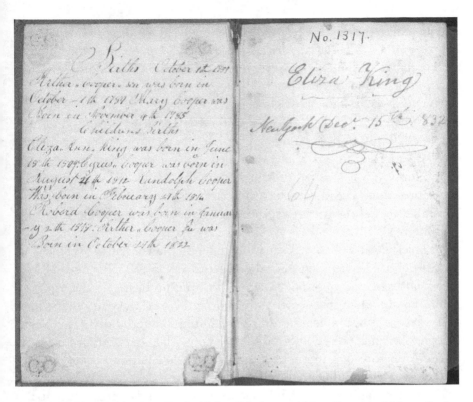

The King Bible provides dates for the births of Arthur and Mary Cooper's children. *Courtesy of Nantucket Historical Association.*

part of the District of Columbia. Historian Kathryn Grover identified the *Regulator* as a flour packet out of New Bedford, Massachusetts, captained by Samuel Chadwick. The sloop was returning to New Bedford carrying not only flour. It was also carrying the stolen human property for which, as Fairfax court orders attest, Captain Chadwick was later accused of trying to defraud and deprive the owner. The *Regulator* belonged to John Avery Parker, a wealthy New Bedford businessman, and Weston Howland, son of the grain and flour mogul of New Bedford.

By the time Camillus Griffith was pursuing the Coopers in 1822, about four years had passed since their escape on the *Regulator*. When they fled, Randolph and the Coopers had been enslaved at Hancock Lee's plantation in Fairfax County, in northern Virginia, a county where slavery had been entrenched for two centuries. Although more up-to-date farmers were trying to replenish the exhausted soil and were replacing tobacco with grain as a cash crop, others still grew tobacco. By 1810, the slave trade in "surplus" county enslaved labor had begun, frightening local bondsmen. In 1820, the county had 4,673 enslaved African Americans, 41 percent of the county's total population, though they were concentrated more densely around Truro Parish, where Hancock Lee lived.

Hancock was a name passed on in the extensive Lee family. "Hancock Lee" is mentioned in Fairfax censuses for 1810 with seventeen bondsmen and in 1820 with eight bondsmen. This mention may refer to either a father who was married to Sinah and who died in 1811 or a son who inherited from him who was married to Mary Nicholson. Griffith may have said he was representing David Ricketts as the current owner of "George" and his family because of the younger Hancock Lee's debts leading to the sale of his "surplus labor" in absentia.

Nantucket could not have been more different than Virginia. Weather was the least of it. Massachusetts had abolished slavery in 1783. Even so, African American residents were not isolated from the problems of the enslaved in the South. They still had friends and family in slavery in other states. Some sailors also experienced discrimination in southern ports. The Negro Seamen Acts first passed in South Carolina in 1822 and then in Louisiana forced African American sailors to stay in jail while in port because of fear of their dangerous influence on those enslaved.

Nantucket was a barren island, isolated by water and forced to look to the sea for its livelihood. Like New Bedford, where Randolph settled, Nantucket was a whaling port with Quaker and African American communities welcoming freedom seekers. As ports, both New Bedford and Nantucket had a variety of jobs for African Americans as seamen or in shore trades and businesses associated with the sea. Nantucket whaling captains needed more sailors than the island could supply by itself. Besides, whaling ships were good places to hide, far from pursuers, with racial equality in treatment and in profit at the end of the voyage. In 1820, there were 247 African Americans on Nantucket to welcome the Coopers. Because the Quakers on Nantucket had eschewed slavery in the 1700s, some African American Nantucketers had been free for more than one generation. Leading Nantucket African Americans like Edward J. Pompey and Absalom Boston had emerged as ship captains and shopkeepers.

After their rescue, Mary and Arthur Cooper were content to remain on Nantucket until their deaths in 1826 and 1852, respectively. During the lifetime of the adult Coopers, there were opportunities for an African American man. Arthur could prosper and be a leader on Nantucket despite inequality and prejudice. In 1830, Arthur appears on the U.S. Census as head of a

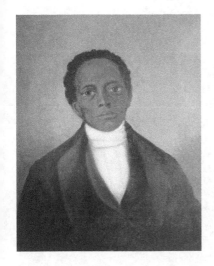

Arthur Cooper is the subject of a folk-art-style portrait painted by Sarah Gardner in about 1830. *Courtesy of Nantucket Historical Association.*

household of seven (presumably including his wife and five children); he continues to appear as head of the household until 1850. This notation is important, because many African Americans began their work careers as domestic servants living in their employers' houses. While working, Arthur was able to save money, whether it was while he was a laborer (U.S. Census) or a labor scout for whaling ships in the 1840s (as noted in a deposition). His savings were enough to buy the house on Angola Street in 1833 and to become a founder of the Zion African Methodist Episcopal Church. This church, incorporated in 1835, was the one for which he would become an elder.

By the time of his death, Arthur Cooper had attained significant leadership in advancing African American rights on Nantucket. He had been president of a convention opposing African American colonization in 1834, and his name appeared on petitions. The petitions discovered so far are from 1838, 1843 and 1845—in 1843 to Congress to abolish slavery and to end legal slave trade in D.C., and in 1838 and 1845 to the state legislature to, respectively, end discrimination on the basis of color and integrate education. Someone else may have actually signed for him. Arthur may not have become literate, as he marked his will with an *X* instead of signing it, but he clearly appreciated education, running for the school committee unsuccessfully in 1842 and being part of the struggle to integrate Nantucket's schools in the 1840s.

A neighbor who was the author of an 1878 letter to the editor of the *Nantucket Inquirer* remembered Arthur as an "industrious, nice, quiet man, also exemplary in a Christian life." His reputation lived on. A 1936 article states, "He lived an honorable life, devoted to the colored folk of the island which had saved him from slavery."

The African American community has not provided its version of the rescue story, as Nantucketers, African American and white, left in search of opportunities not offered by Nantucket's declining whaling industry. Arthur and Mary's son Randolph ended up in San Jose, California. Arthur Jr., a barber in Nantucket, sailed on the ship *Aurora* to the California goldfields and

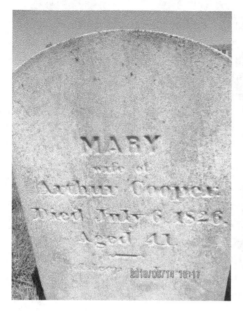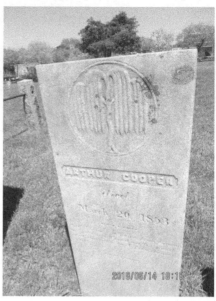

Left: Mary Cooper is buried beside her husband. *Right*: Arthur Cooper's grave is his commemoration on Nantucket. *Jenny Masur.*

later became a steward on a ship to Hawaii. The most significant reminder of the African American history the rescue represents is the Coloured Cemetery behind Nantucket Cottage Hospital. It is the burial site of Arthur, Arthur's first wife, Mary, and Arthur's second wife, Lucy.

The escape story of the Coopers is one that ended up as a resounding success. It was forgotten in Virginia but became part of a proud community tradition of tolerance and abolitionism in Nantucket, where the descendants of white participants and nineteenth- and twentieth-century newspapers and island historians kept the tradition alive. The story reflects the Yankee virtues of thrift—a version of the surviving story tells that it was not necessary to pay a purchase price for Arthur Cooper in order to protect him. One version highlights the local value given to education by claiming that Quakers taught Arthur to read and write. Or, as one Nantucketer put it, the story is one of the "manliness and grit" of the magistrates and freemen. Above all, the Coopers' story is a story of Yankee independence.

The incident was reported in the newspaper in 1822–23 and in testimony at Griffith's trial in Boston. Then it reappears in local newspapers at the end of the nineteenth century. The gap is attributed to the silence thought apt because of the general public disapproval of abolitionists. The story's

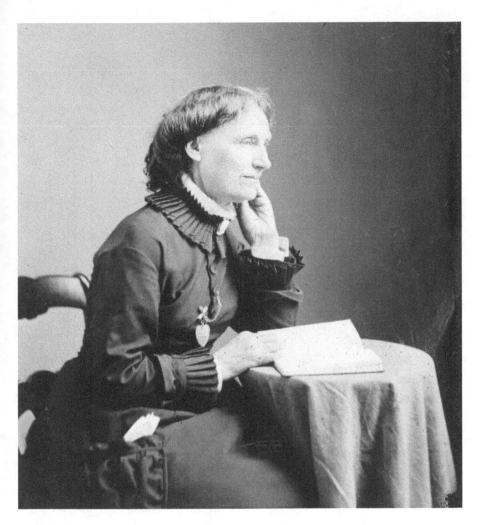

Anna Gardner taught black children, first in Nantucket and then in Charlottesville, Virginia. *Courtesy of Nantucket Historical Association.*

later telling fits the model of the Underground Railroad stories that emerged after the Civil War as whites began to claim Underground Railroad history. Various prominent white families took credit for leadership and for providing a hiding place—Folgers, Macys, Gardners, Mitchells— depending on the version. For example, Anna Gardner was six years old at the time that Arthur hid in her parents' house. She was profoundly affected, and her memory was imprinted with a visual image of terrified Arthur. She repeatedly insisted the experience led to her later career as an abolitionist and a teacher of African

American children, first in Nantucket's segregated African American school and, after the Civil War, in a school in Charlottesville, Virginia. She repeated a consistent story to her family, to a friend in Charlottesville who kept a journal and to the island newspaper.

Nonetheless, over time, some details have become fuzzy. Depending on the source, the house to which the Coopers fled is claimed as the Folgers', and/or the Gardners' and/or the Mitchells'. Perhaps because the tradition has been passed down by white islanders, agency tends to be given to the white leaders, not the African American crowd and the Coopers. All accounts, however, concur that the African American crowd was present before the whites arrived.

The original version does not explain how the freedom seekers were traced from Virginia to Nantucket, although an article in the *Inquirer and Mirror* of January 25, 1936, attributes responsibility to a Virginia Underground Railroad informer. Notwithstanding the indictment of Chadwick in Fairfax for carrying away the Coopers on the *Regulator*, a version says they left from Norfolk. Arthur is always the protagonist, but sometimes it is only Mary with whom he flees, or only Mary and one child. According to his age in a later census, Randolph would have been that child. Sometimes, Arthur is the focus of the slave catchers, as Mary and the children are said to be free. Indeed, some versions replace Mary with Lucy, his second wife, who lived to a ripe old age.

Arthur Cooper and his family are heroes in Nantucket, although they are unknown elsewhere. In fact, in Nantucket, the story is iconic, standing for the tolerance and respect for others exercised by its people.

2

ANNA MARIA GANT

From Loudoun County to Zanesville

A nna Maria Hughes Gant, a "mulato" woman, died on October 11, 1877, while visiting her married daughter in Yorktown, Virginia. She was only fifty but worn out by twelve pregnancies in thirty years. The unhealthy climate in Yorktown and heart disease compounded the "tinges" of fever she had felt before leaving home in Zanesville, Ohio.

Nothing remains of Anna Maria's history in her own words. Her husband, Nelson T. Gant, dedicated a monument to her in Woodlawn Cemetery in Zanesville as a testament to their love. It was only after Maria's death that Nelson gave newspaper interviews revealing the romantic part of the Gants' life. He or the writer may have embellished the story. What confirming information there is regarding Anna Maria's life comes from family tradition and from what can be gleaned from legal documents, censuses and tax records. Luckily, there is a descendant engaged in dogged research of the details of Nelson and Anna Maria Gant's lives.

"Maria Gant," as she was known in Zanesville, was given the honor of a eulogy reprinted in the *Christian Recorder* on April 11, 1878. It was given by the preeminent African Methodist Episcopal bishop Daniel Payne, who described her as one sustained by religious beliefs. In her teen years, she went to Sunday school at the Leesburg Methodist Church. She retained her faith in her later years as an active member of St. Paul's African Methodist Episcopal Church in Zanesville. The bishop proclaimed her as "zealous of good works" for the church, the poor and the needy regardless of background. He praised her as "one who, though weary with the toll of many years, and worn with labors which knew no hours, was ever ready to do a friendly act, or go on an errand of mercy."

Maria Gant died half a century old, having lived through years of remarkable change. Slavery had ended, and opportunities, albeit limited, were available to former bondsmen. Salient points of her life—slavery, escape to freedom, transition to prosperity and deaths of children—may have been taken for granted by African Americans of her time. The bishop did not feel it necessary to do more than praise her virtues inspired by her faith. It was not necessary to speak of the tragic loss of her children in a time of high infant mortality. He may have considered it not luck but the grace of God that she found a good man and brought him to God. The bishop did not bother to mention her virtues in a woman's sphere—managing a household, being a good helpmate to her husband, bringing up children and showing hospitality to guests. To him, her life in slavery was secondary. Her escape from slavery was apparently not unusual. She herself, however, would not have overlooked the blessing of living long enough to achieve liberty. After she was free and situated in Zanesville, she must have daily marveled at living in freedom and in a prosperity of her and her husband's making.

The eulogy, written during a generation filled with ex-slaves and certain assumptions about women, left certain details out. Not mentioned were Maria's children. She raised four children in freedom and saw her grandchildren born as free citizens. By the time her daughters and son were the age when she herself had received freedom, she and her husband could afford to treat them like young ladies and gentlemen. They lived a life comparable to that of a wealthy white farmer's children. Their large farm would have been the pride of any man—African American or white—in the county. They enjoyed rosewood furniture in the parlor. Her daughters studied music like the white slaveholders' daughters of her youth. The son and two daughters went to study at Oberlin College, a school open to African American and white, male and female. She saw her daughters well married. It would have seemed amazing that Sadie was married to Daniel McNorton, a freedom seeker who after the Civil War became a senator in the Virginia General Assembly and a physician. Pride in her Lizzie (Elizabeth), Sadie (Sarah), Maggie (Margaret) and Nelson Jr. had to be balanced with grief for the other eight children who never grew up. Among them were little Theodora, who died at five months old, Henrietta at ten months old and two she lost in 1860—little Benjamin (only four days old) and Alice (already five years old). This grief was the counterpoint to the joy given her by her four surviving children.

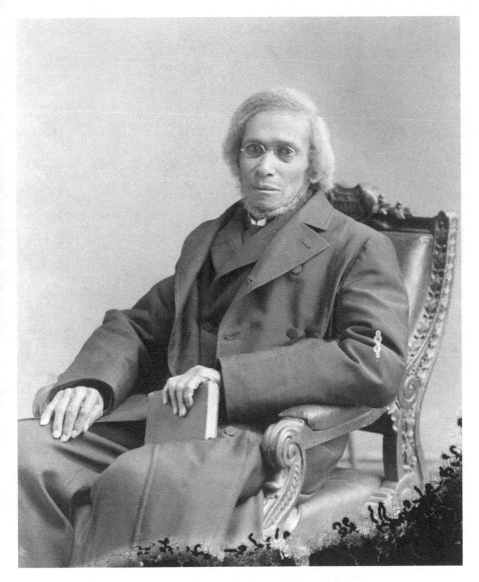

Bishop D.A. Payne was a friend of the Gants. *Library of Congress.*

One of Maria Gant's most cherished possessions surely was her certificate of freedom. Unforgettably, she grew up in slavery in Loudoun County, Virginia, where she was born about 1826. She was one of the group of enslaved women and children given to the three Russell sisters by their mother, Sarah Elizabeth McCarty Russell. Sarah Russell was a proud

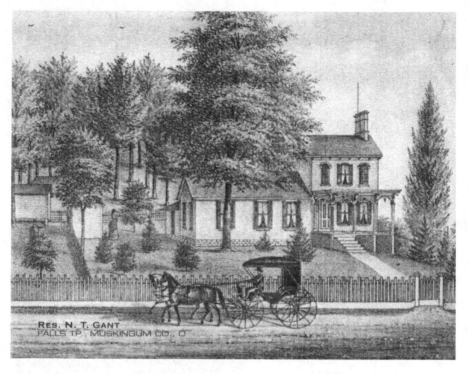

RES. N. T. GANT
FALLS TP., MUSKINGUM CO., O

The Gant Homestead had this appearance toward the end of Nelson Gant's life.
Combination Atlas Map of Muskingum County, Ohio, *Everts & Co., 1875.*

second cousin of George Washington, and Maria only chattel. Maria spent long hours during her teens working as a house servant in Leesburg, surely despairing of ever escaping her lot as a source of endless unpaid labor.

Maria found Nelson Talbot Gant while they were both still in slavery in Virginia. He was her husband by the law of God and the father of her twelve children. Even toward the end of his life, Nelson was still a fine figure—more than six feet tall and two hundred pounds, as described in "Rivals Romance" in the *Zanesville Courier* of November 17, 1894. The article went on to say that he was well spoken and could converse "fluently, using as good English as an individual of ordinary education." He was a man with friends like the great African American orator, publisher and statesman Frederick Douglass.

Maria's ongoing love for her husband was unusual in an era when owners could arrange and break up marriages at will. If being enslaved was not unusual, it must have been so to choose her husband, have a preacher marry them with consent of their owners and retain her husband in the transition to freedom.

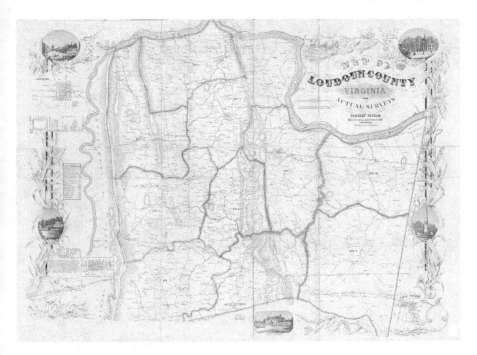

This "Map of Loudoun County, VA," was drawn by Underground Railroad operative Yardley Taylor in about 1854. *Library of Congress.*

"Talbott," as her husband was called in slavery (also spelled Talbot or Talbert), was shrewd and hardworking, a man of integrity. Maria spent more than thirty years at his side, for better and for worse, as his source of comfort and his mainstay. After only fifteen years of freedom, he had a 180-acre farm. As Nelson later liked to say, he came to Zanesville with $0.50 in his pocket and was eventually worth $55,000. As one of Zanesville's richest men, he came to own a three-hundred-acre farm, a salt lick and a coal mine. From the beginning, Maria helped as she could despite her pregnancies, the upbringing and illnesses of her children and household chores. She was at Nelson's side for the five years he was a hired gardener and then while he was starting and building a wholesale market gardening business. Even as he became more prosperous from selling fruits and vegetables harvested early, she helped as she could. For example, she sold strawberries and cream from the porch. From slavery through freedom, she worked without respite, but in Zanesville, she was subject only to the whims and fancies of her husband and children.

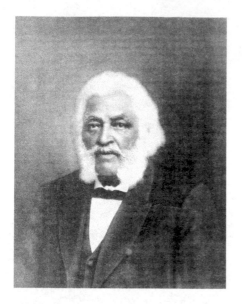

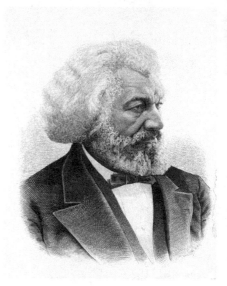

Left: Nelson Gant became a prosperous and prominent citizen of Zanesville. *1905 History Past and Present of the City of Zanesville & Muskingum County, Ohio*, by J. Hope Sutor. *Courtesy of Muskingum County Chapter, Ohio Genealogical Society.*

Right: Frederick Douglass was a self-taught genius who became the most prominent African American of the nineteenth century. *Library of Congress.*

May 11, the day after Maria's husband's birthday, was their special day, the day on which they remembered their marriage in 1843 by a minister from Leesburg Methodist Church. Perhaps Talbott and Maria met through Maria's Sunday school classmate Winifred Jane, since she was owned by the same man as Talbott. Maria and Talbott had in common that they were both house servants—she a maid and he a valet for his owner. She lived in Leesburg, but Woodburn Estate, where he lived, was a little outside the city. The distance between them was not too far for courting. When they wanted to marry, marriage was not an easy proposition. A couple like Maria and Talbott could not marry legally or without permission of their owners, who were not easily persuaded. But Maria and Talbott were married.

After only two years of marriage, Talbott's love was tested when he was freed by the will of his owner, John Nixon. An antislavery Quaker preacher, possibly Lucretia Mott, had visited Leesburg in 1842. Although a slaveholder, Nixon had been greatly impressed by meeting and hearing her speak. He changed his will to free his twenty-two bondsmen and -women. The will stipulated that not only were they to be freed, but they also were to be provided transport to Zanesville, Ohio, and two plots of land, one for each matriarch in the group.

After Talbott was emancipated in September 1845, he became "Nelson Talbot(t) Gant" on legal documents. He had a new identity and a new future. Maria, however, was still enslaved. She had a different owner, who did not heed Talbott's request for her freedom so that she could accompany him. When the others freed by Nixon left, Talbott stayed behind to earn enough to buy Maria's freedom. Unfortunately, Virginia law provided him only one year before forcing him to leave the state. That did not allow him enough time to earn sufficient money. He appeared propertyless in the 1846 county personal property tax records.

Talbott had to leave for Ohio but pledged he would return. Maria could not know whether he would fulfill his promise of returning for her within six weeks. It was an anxious period of her life. She was ready to forsake her family and friends to find freedom with Talbott but could not know if she could count on him.

Somehow, Talbott managed. He returned, determined to free her by one means or another. He had used the intervening time to establish Underground Railroad contacts. From later events, it was clear that he knew Austin A. Guthrie and other antislavery advocates from the abolitionist hotbed of Putnam (near Zanesville) in Ohio. A letter Talbott wrote on June 7, 1847, describes how he stayed at the house of Dr. Francis Julius LeMoyne, an Underground operative in Washington County, Pennsylvania. The letter mentions that he somehow met Martin Delaney, an African American activist in Pittsburgh who went on to become the first African American field officer in the U.S. Army during the Civil War. Talbott's contacts enabled him to pull together what he thought would be enough money to redeem Maria's freedom and bring her to live with him in Zanesville.

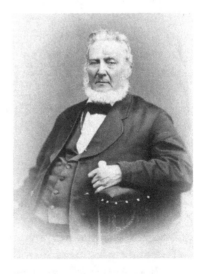

Dr. Francis J. LeMoyne sheltered Nelson Gant as Gant plotted the escape of his wife, Maria. *Library of Congress.*

When Talbott returned to Leesburg, Maria's owner again turned down his request to purchase Maria's freedom. Talbott was prepared. Just in case the purchase money did not persuade Maria's owner, Talbott had procured counterfeit papers for her so they could flee together through the assistance of his Underground Railroad friends.

By October 10, 1846, Maria and Talbott were together, but in jail in Washington, D.C. They had been betrayed. Years later, Nelson told a reporter how Maria had left from the home of a sympathetic neighbor of her owner's, the Loudoun County clerk, Charles G. Eskridge. Eskridge only belatedly informed Miss Russell that Maria had run away three days earlier. That delay gave Maria time to get to Washington to meet Talbott. After they met up, they mistakenly trusted another "coloured" man. They were found, and Maria's papers were judged useless.

Maria's owner, Charlye Ann Elizabeth Jane Russell, petitioned the Virginia governor to extradite the couple back to Leesburg from D.C. Talbott had a brief court appearance during which he was defended by Thomas Carlisle and well-known lawyer General Walter Jones. These lawyers were well qualified but could not prevent his extradition to Virginia because to slaveholders he represented a menace. In late October 1846, Talbott was taken to the Leesburg jail by the Virginia governor's order to stand trial. He was charged with "carrying" Maria out of state in order to "defraud" and "deprive" her owner of Maria's $500 value.

The two had a lot at stake in the December 1846 trial of Talbott. Maria could continue in slavery, and Talbott could be imprisoned or re-enslaved and sold out of state. While Talbott and Maria waited for the trial, they were both under great pressure to confess to collusion. Maria in particular had to stay silent about Talbott's role and claim she had fled without him. Since she was back in slavery, Maria could be coerced to testify against him, for instance, with a threat of sale south. She stood fast with the knowledge that Talbott had risked his freedom for hers.

Fortunately, Thomas Nichols intervened. Nichols had been the executor of John Nixon's will and had accompanied most of the Nixon freedmen and women to Zanesville. Nichols knew the respected Leesburg lawyer John Janney and persuaded him to defend Talbott with the assistance of Robert P. Swann and James S. Carper. The trial had to wait until Commonwealth Attorney Burr William Harrison succeeded in bringing in needed witnesses.

There are no transcripts of the trial, but the *National Era* of January 7, 1847, the *Christian Register* of January 30, 1847, and the *New York Evangelist* of February 11, 1847, reported the lawyers' legal arguments. Hearteningly for the Gants, defense attorney Swann began the trial by recognizing Talbott as equal to whites in his feelings, with "a heart beating within his body, and a soul that is capable of the tenderest emotions." Swann eloquently argued that Talbott was a man "united in holy wedlock to a woman for whom he has evinced the strongest feelings of attachment." A slave marriage was never recognized in court, so it must have been quite a moment to hear Swann say that Maria and Talbott had been "married in the chancery of heaven."

When called to testify, Maria responded bravely to John Janney's questions by saying "that she was married to the prisoner, three years ago, in her mistress's house, with her consent by" a minister. Her lawyer, Carper, sprang up to protest that if she were married, she did not have to testify and that if she were enslaved she could not testify freely. His arguments worked. The trial climaxed in a glorious moment when the panel of judges decided to recognize their marriage and not require Maria's testimony. Not surprisingly, the Washington paper the *National Era* noted that Maria was "much delighted" by the decision. The only other witness called was a hesitant African American man whose statements were discounted. Talbott was discharged by the court. The *National Era* called it "an interesting and important decision" for the precedent it set.

After the trial, Talbott was released from jail, but Maria remained in bondage. Talbott prevailed upon Miss Russell to let him redeem Maria, reminding her that she had given permission for their marriage. She relented. In a letter to Dr. Francis Julius LeMoyne on June 7, 1847, Talbott related that Thomas Nichols and other Quakers along with Gant's brother-in-law had loaned them money. The couple had needed $975 to purchase Maria's freedom and to pay the costs of the lawsuit.

That left Maria and Talbott the task of paying back their lenders. It took them much more than the year permitted to remain in Virginia by state law. By staying the extra time, Talbott had hanging over his head an

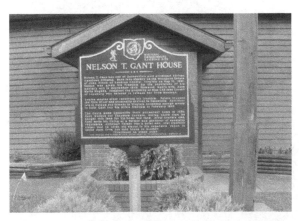

A Gant marker presently stands by the Gant home. *Anita Jackson.*

indictment that he received in 1848 and that was continued until 1850. Meanwhile, John Janney and Thomas Nichols did not forget Talbott and Maria. According to tax records, Talbott lived for three years with a friend of Nichols' and a cousin of Janney's. He was Samuel Janney, another Quaker from Goose Creek Meeting in Loudoun County and a known friend of the African American community. Talbott worked catering for Janney's boarding school.

Having paid off the loan and avoided arrest, the couple left Loudoun County in June 1850, finally reaching freedom in Zanesville. They could begin to work for themselves and their growing family and to show the height of prosperity and prominence a family of ex-bondsmen could achieve. They and their love are now commemorated by a marker and a wayside exhibit.

3

ANN MARIA WEEMS

From Montgomery County to Canada

To Ann Maria Weems, an impatient teenage girl in slavery, freedom could not come soon enough. She had been waiting and waiting while years went by, the last of John and Arrah Weems' daughters in slavery. Her sister Catherine had been redeemed and recorded free at D.C. City Hall, and her sister Mary Jane had fled to freedom with her aunt and uncle and their children. That left Ann Maria waiting for her turn beginning at age twelve.

William Still recorded the Weems saga in which he had participated in his book *The Underground Railroad*. The Weems family consisted of a free father, John, an enslaved mother, Arrah (Airy), three daughters and five sons. They were living together in Rockville, Maryland, as happily as a family in slavery could live, when they received a shock in 1847. Arrah's owner, Adam Robb, died. That meant that annual payments to Robb and his promise to sell the Weems family to John were no longer enough to keep the family together. The family alternately must have hoped and despaired during the hiatus of probate after Robb's death. They had to contemplate fearfully the sale of individual members of the family, dividing and dispersing the Weemses into more brutal situations.

John Weems had to act as quickly as he could. He appealed to Jacob Bigelow, the white D.C. Underground Railroad operative, and at the same time also acted on his own. Bigelow, a Massachusetts-born lawyer ostensibly associated with the Washington gas company, had inherited the management of Underground Railroad operations from William Chaplin in 1850. Like

Chaplin, he was part of a biracial network that extended to Lewis Tappan, the New York philanthropist, and vigilance committees in New York and Philadelphia.

Having accumulated only $400 of the $900 needed to purchase the first family members, in the early 1850s, John Weems took two trips to New York City. He was hoping to enlist the help of his eldest daughter, Mary Jane, who had already taken flight for freedom. He was disappointed to learn that she was not in New York. Persisting, John found out from Reverend Charles Bennett Ray of the New York Vigilance Committee that his daughter was in England. Now called "Stella," she was with the family of her foster father, Henry Highland Garnet. Reverend Garnet was a former freedom seeker from Maryland who had become a distinguished clergyman and abolitionist lecturer. In order to help John, Ray wrote to Garnet, with whose family Stella had been living for two years. Until leaving Great Britain for Jamaica in November 1852, Garnet was in a position to spread news of the family's plight through his lectures and articles. In 1853, donations by sympathetic contributors created the Weems Ransom Fund (eventually $5,000), with Henry and Anna Richardson, English abolitionists, as treasurers.

The money, however, did not reach Underground Railroad operative Jacob Bigelow in time to prevent the sale and separation of the Weems family. On his return from the North, John Weems found that Adam Robb's heirs had decided to pay off debts by selling their bondsmen. Ann Maria, along with her sister Catherine, were now the property of the slave trader Charles Price of Unity, Maryland. Ann Maria's mother and five brothers were awaiting sale in Washington Jail. Family fears of separation were realized when the big group was sold to Montgomery, Alabama. The news reached across the seas. The entire family's suffering was barely imaginable, despite newspaper descriptions. Stella was reported to be brokenhearted. The British public was touched, and the fund grew.

Because Bigelow was a lawyer, he could represent the family and begin negotiating with those who had purchased the Weems family members. The sum of $1,600 from the Weems Ransom Fund was enough to allow Arrah and the two youngest sons to return to live in freedom with John in Washington. Sixteen and attractive, Catherine was at risk of purchase for sexual exploitation, so the remaining $1,600 bought her freedom.

Bigelow, however, balked at Price's exaggerated price for Ann Maria, also a budding young woman. From the time Ann Maria was twelve, Price had refused the offer of $700 from her would-be rescuers. Instead, he waited— presumably for an even more exaggerated price of $1,000 from either the

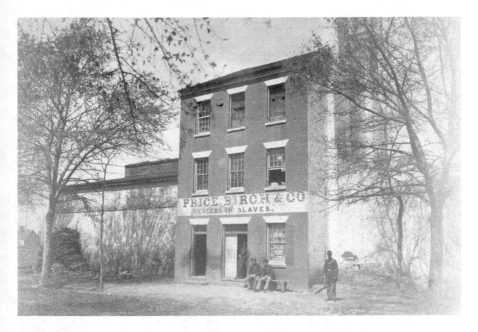

The Price, Birch & Co. slave jail in Alexandria, Virginia, shown in 1861, survives as the Northern Virginia Urban League. *Library of Congress.*

lawyer's backers or from a lascivious buyer. In a quandary, Jacob Bigelow had one option left if he were to help the Weems. From New York, Reverend Charles Ray wrote to urge him to abandon legal means and enable Ann Maria to run away.

While Ann Maria waited and Bigelow stewed, arrangements dragged on. Ann Maria could not escape easily, because her suspicious owner was careful, having her sleep in his and his wife's bedroom. Even if Ann Maria could escape, in the rescuers' eyes she still was too young to travel unescorted over the ten or so miles between Rockville, Maryland, and Washington. In Washington, she would need refuge and money to pay her expenses while hidden. Because staying with her family in Washington would not be safe, she would have to travel first to a state across the Mason-Dixon line and then to Canada, where she had an aunt and uncle enjoying the freedom offered there by the British.

Coded letters traveled back and forth in 1854 and 1855 among Bigelow, William Still of the Philadelphia Vigilance Committee and Reverend Charles Ray of the New York Vigilance Committee. Precious time was wasted in the summer of 1855 while Still was on another mission away from Philadelphia. Options were proposed and dismissed as too risky to have Ann

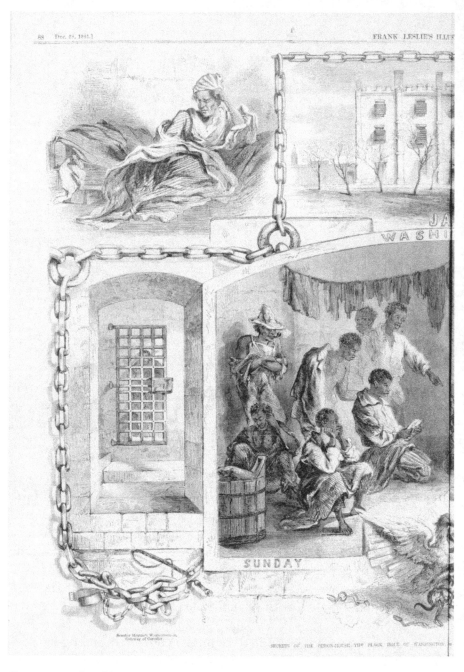

Controversy reigned because the D.C. Jail housed bondsmen. *Frank Leslie's Illustrated Newspaper*, December 29, 1861. *Library of Congress.*

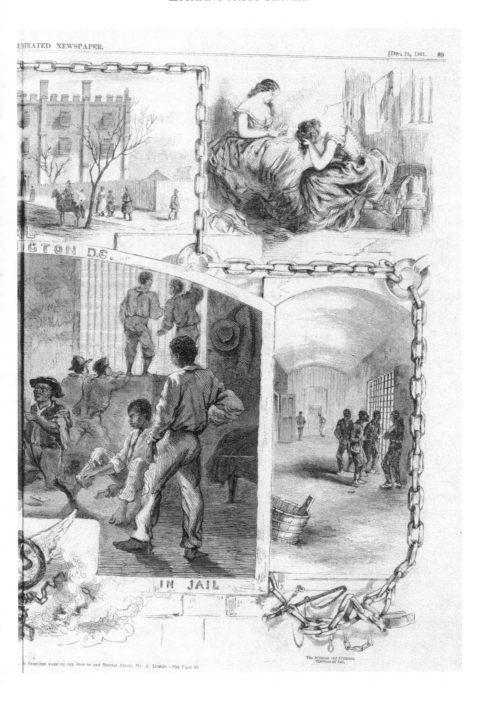

Maria escorted north by her mother, Arrah, and Bigelow or by her two young cousins. The Philadelphia Vigilance Committee proposed and, in 1855, dispatched to Bigelow a ship's captain whose code name was "Powder Boy." Powder Boy apparently was disinclined to participate on account of what Bigelow called the "little light freight" and by the lack of an advance—such money would have had to be channeled through the Richardsons in England and Lewis Tappan in New York.

As an alternative, the Philadelphia Vigilance Committee proposed that an unidentified "professional gentleman" convey Ann Maria by carriage to avoid slave catchers lurking around the D.C. railroad station. Given the gentleman's anonymity, Bigelow was cautious and made a fall 1854 visit to Underground Railroad contact William Wright near Gettysburg, Pennsylvania. Wright identified the escort as Dr. Ellwood Harvey, a professor at the Female Medical College of Pennsylvania in Philadelphia. Dr. Harvey, Still later assured Bigelow, was someone with antislavery credentials. When Bigelow finally met Harvey, Bigelow was immediately reassured. He reinforced Dr. Harvey's antislavery beliefs with the offer of $300, a sum Harvey needed to buy equipment for his medical school.

At last, Ann Maria had an opportunity to escape to D.C. In October 1855, Bigelow wrote to William Still in Philadelphia that "the poor, timid, breathless, flying child of fifteen" had escaped from Charles Price on September 23. Her owner was angry enough to place an ad for the incredible sum of $500 in the *Baltimore Sun* on October 2, 1855.

Ann Maria needed to travel north sooner rather than later, but Dr. Harvey was unable to get away from his professorial duties yet. That left Ann Maria

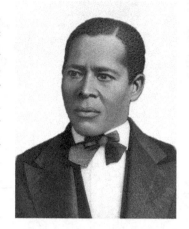

William Still was a member of the Philadelphia Vigilance Committee and took notes on arrivals fleeing from slavery. *Library of Congress.*

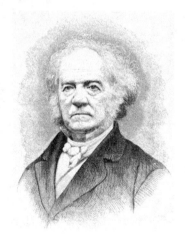

Lewis Tappan supplied funds for Underground Railroad operations. *Library of Congress.*

$500 REWARD.—Ran away on Sunday night, the 23d instant, before 12 o'clock, from the subscriber, residing in Rockville, Montgomery county, Md., my NEGRO GIRL "Ann Maria Weems," about 15 years of age; a bright mulatto; some small freckles on her face; slender person, thick suit of hair, inclined to be sandy. Her parents are free, and reside in Washington, D. C. It is evident she was taken away by some one in a carriage, probably by a white man, by whom she may be carried beyond the limits of the State of Maryland.

I will give the above reward for her apprehension and detention so that I get her again.

s27-d4m&4tW; **C. M. PRICE.**

The runaway ad for Ann Maria Weems gives a physical description and suspected getaway. *Collection of the Maryland State Archives.*

and her protectors in D.C. vulnerable to relentless slave hunters and greedy informers. Bigelow rightly worried over taking sufficient precautions to avoid fines and prison for himself and sale south for Ann Maria. Bigelow made his letters to Still more cryptic and used the pseudonym "William Penn."

Price guessed the manner and direction she would use to escape, but he did not foresee that Ann Maria would hide in D.C. while pursuers searched the usual routes out of Rockville and Washington. Ann Maria's eight weeks of waiting in hiding were not wasted. Bigelow spent them transforming Ann Maria into a boy named "Joe Wright." Ann Maria had to carry herself convincingly as a boy and hide her girl's hair. She had to accustom herself to wearing a boy's clothes and cap.

The day of escape was set by Still. Ann Maria had to wait no longer. The doctor rented a horse and carriage in Baltimore and arrived in D.C. at the meeting place. The White House had been chosen as the place so that it would seem that Dr. Harvey had just made a house call to the presidential mansion. Playing the role of Dr. Harvey's coachman, Ann Maria grabbed the reins and whip while Bigelow and Harvey were saying goodbye. At the doctor's order to proceed, they drove off.

Once Harvey and "Joe Wright" were sufficiently far away, the more experienced doctor took over driving the carriage. He wanted to be ready for any dangers. At the turnpike gates, the pair had to bluff a suspicious toll keeper who did not want to let them through. Farther along, there was a reluctant ferry operator to persuade. By evening, they had successfully arrived at the farm of an old acquaintance of Dr. Harvey's, a slaveholder. The doctor anticipated that they would be invited to spend the night and rest and feed the horse.

To justify his sudden appearance at the farm, Dr. Harvey claimed that he was bolstering his health with a drive to reconnect with familiar faces and landscapes. He stifled his political views while he acted the part of a distinguished gentleman well past any youthful indiscretions like helping a

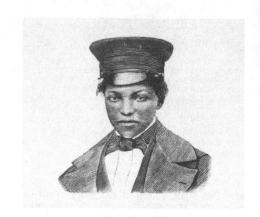

Right: Ann Maria Weems escaped disguised as a boy. *New York Public Library*.

Below: A street scene by the White House, circa 1850. The Willard Hotel, which still exists, is in the foreground. *Library of Congress*.

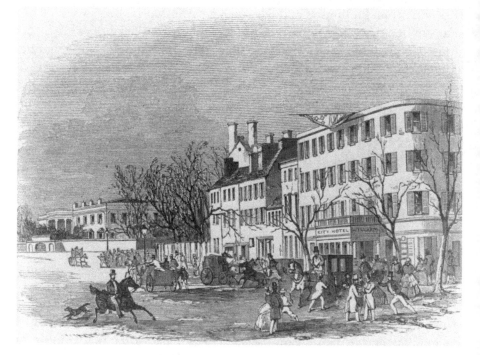

freedom seeker. While Joe sheltered in the kitchen, the doctor enjoyed the farmer's hospitality in the parlor. Harvey made convincing conversation about agriculture and slaveholding and fended off jokes about Joe as a possible runaway. That night, to avoid discovery, the doctor claimed he needed to have Joe close at hand, so Joe slept wrapped in a quilt in a corner of Dr. Harvey's bedroom.

Expeditiously, Dr. Harvey and Joe Wright made an early start the next morning, and the next day or night crossed the Mason-Dixon line. They had traversed Maryland successfully, but crossing the Susquehanna River to Philadelphia was almost their undoing—it took a literal show of strength by the doctor, who was tall, large and broad-shouldered, to keep a group of men from interfering with their travels.

By 4:00 p.m. on November 22, 1855, the two had arrived at William Still's home in Philadelphia. As the Stills' family doctor, Dr. Harvey could legitimately stop at their home. As William Still later described the scene, Harvey dropped off Joe (his "packet") while announcing to Mrs. Still in passing, "I wish to leave this young lad with you a short while." Mrs. Still had not yet discovered the identity of the "boy" when her husband arrived. Heeding the doctor's instructions, Joe had been cautious about divulging her identity as Ann Maria until Joe and William Still were alone.

In order to rest, Ann Maria passed her first couple of days of freedom with the Stills. The breathtaking novelty of freedom was accompanied by the unique experience of sitting for a daguerreotype for her mother and for Still's files. Ann Maria herself was a novelty to the members of the vigilance committee and others privileged to meet her. The story of a girl escaping disguised as a boy was intriguing. Northeast antislavery kingpin Lewis Tappan worried about disclosing the details to too many people and so destroying the possibility of re-use of the same strategy.

The disguise had been a success from Maryland to Philadelphia, but Ann Maria had not yet reached her destination of Canada and legal freedom. Already a series of conspirators had been involved—Bigelow, Dr. Harvey, Still and Reverend Ray. Reverend Ray was the next link on the Underground Railroad responsible for escorting Ann Maria to Canada. He was not surprised by her sudden appearance, writing that when "one afternoon upon arriving home I found, sitting on the sofa at my house, a little boy about ten years old in appearance and looking rather feminine. I knew at once who it was…Joe."

There was an opportunity for all those involved to express gratitude for their luck so far. On Wednesday, November 28, Reverend Ray accompanied Ann Maria dressed as Joe to the Brooklyn home of Lewis Tappan. As described by the Tappans in a letter, the celebration of Thanksgiving in the Tappans' house was truly a day for giving thanks. Ann Maria and the Tappans alike exulted over her achievement of freedom. Still at risk of pursuit, she sat in a locked room in her Joe disguise poised for immediate flight. While family and friends celebrated downstairs, upstairs, Ann Maria ate her turkey and plum pudding in glorious freedom. Trusted celebrants enjoyed her smile when they came up to see how she was.

Tappan was in a hurry to get Ann Maria safely to southwestern Ontario, where she had the uncle and aunt who had escaped four years earlier with her sister Stella (Mary Jane). After the Fugitive Slave Act of 1850, the aunt and uncle, now using their freedom names of William Henry and Annie Bradley, had fled from Geneva, New York, where they and Stella had settled. Their destination was the African American refugee colony of Buxton, Ontario, which had been founded and sustained with money provided by antislavery Britons and New Englanders.

Within two days of Ann Maria's arrival, Tappan's wife, Sarah, outfitted for Ann Maria a trunk filled with a girl's clothes, "warm and strong...[for] Canada." But, when Ann Maria was on her way, she had an unanticipated escort in place of Reverend Ray. She was accompanied by Reverend Amos Freeman. Reverend Freeman had been a staunch Underground Railroad operative in whatever congregation he presided over, and he was persuaded partly by the offer of a stipend and expenses. After he and Ann Maria left on Friday, no one in New York was at ease until late the next day, when Freeman sent a letter from Niagara Falls. He wrote, "You may judge my joy and relief of mind," when they crossed to Canada over the new Niagara Suspension Bridge.

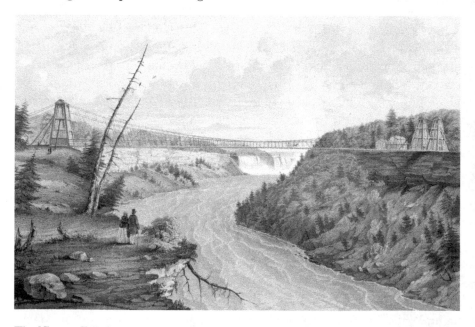

The Niagara Falls Suspension Bridge, built in 1848, marked the border of the United States and Canada. *Library of Congress.*

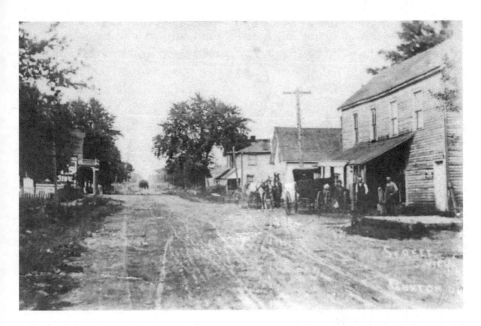

This rare Buxton street scene indicates the kind of home freedom seekers would find in Canada West. *Buxton National Historic Site and Museum.*

In a later letter to Tappan, Reverend Freeman described the rest of the trip before the joyful reunion with Ann Maria's aunt and uncle on December 1. On Saturday night, the travelers reached Chatham, two hundred miles past the border and a place where they were pleased to encounter other freedom seekers. Freeman and Ann Maria had to stop at a boardinghouse to wait until the Sabbath had passed, and there was a wagon available to traverse the remaining sixteen miles of mud.

At the boardinghouse, Freeman could not resist revealing Ann Maria's secret to the host in private. At that point, the host's wife was enlisted to help with Joe's transformation back to the appearance of a girl. It was quite a scene when Ann Maria was reintroduced to the neighbors and boarders present as "Miss Ann Maria Weems," a freedom seeker. All present were flabbergasted and happy, shaking hands with one another, exclaiming and laughing.

On Monday, despite their undoubted impatience, the travelers did not reach the area of the Bradley farm until late. As described by Freeman, he and Ann Maria proceeded on the road there, at last stopping two men for directions. When asked if either knew Bradley, one replied, "'I reckon I am the one that you want to find, my name is Bradley.' Suddenly he caught sight of Ann Maria's face and burst out, 'My Lord! Maria, is that you? Is that you? My child, is it you? We never expected to see you again! We had given you up; O what will your aunt say?'"

Her uncle rushed ahead so that by the time they reached his gate, his wife was tearfully calling out, "Ann Maria, is it you?" Ann Maria jumped from the wagon into her aunt's embrace as they both wept happy tears. Inside, the aunt could not help interrupting the conversation about those still in Maryland with a constant, "My child, you are here! Thank God you are free! We were talking about you today, and saying, we shall never see you again; and now here you are with us." Since the Bradleys' escape, they had waited for four years to be joined by family. Just as they had rejoiced at freedom, they could not help but feel the same joy for Ann Maria. Tappan's wife wrote to the Richardsons that she was sure that Ann Maria would be treated as if she were the aunt and uncle's "own child." The uncle promised that she would get an education, since she could only "read a very little," according to Still's "Journal C." Her uncle further promised that he would try to persuade her parents to come, too. Bradley was eager to share his two farms and his success.

Ann Maria had arrived successfully. Nevertheless, the Weems family saga, which had started in 1847, was not over until 1858. Because of Bigelow's other Underground Railroad duties, rescuing all three remaining brothers in Alabama by purchase of their freedom took from 1856 to 1858. Arrah had to travel to Syracuse and Rochester to raise money; wishing to share her own good fortune, she daringly volunteered to carry a freedom seeker's child to Syracuse. That mother was relieved, but it was not until September 1857 (after sons James and Addison had been purchased and freed) that Ann Maria's mother could write to Still of her joy at the prospect of finally redeeming Augustus for $1,100. Augustus, her last child in slavery in Alabama, was not free until August 1858.

4

EMILY PLUMMER

Going Home in Prince George's County

The Plummer saga is public because Adam Francis Plummer knew how to read and write. Adam not only kept a diary, but letters also circulated among Adam, his wife, Emily, and their children. Nellie Arnold Plummer, the youngest child of Adam and Emily, saved her father's diary and family letters. Having heard many reminiscences by her parents and siblings, Nellie gave insight into the family's thoughts and feelings when she published a book in 1927, *Out of the Depths, or, the Triumph of the Cross*. There is no way to know how the events had been reshaped by the years of retelling. Carter G. Woodson published some Plummer letters in both the *Journal of Negro History* (1926) and *The Mind of the Negro as Reflected in Letters Written During the Crisis 1800–1860* (1926). Interest was revived when the diary annotated by Nellie was given to the Smithsonian's Anacostia Community Museum in 2003 and then placed online.

Despite years of planning and several attempted escapes, freedom came officially for Emily Saunders Plummer and her family only in November 1864, when Maryland changed its state constitution. Attaining freedom by flight was not as easy a gamble for a woman heavily embedded in kinship responsibilities as for a single man. A woman with children had to keep focused on holding the family together while she contemplated freedom. A counterpoint to the yearning for freedom was fear of family separation. Freedom might have to be delayed if the family were to rise united "out of the depths" of slavery, in Nellie's words.

The Adam Plummer Diary refers to Emily's travails. *Anacostia Community Museum, Smithsonian Institution.*

While growing up in slavery at Three Sisters plantation near Bladensburg, Prince George's County, Maryland, Emily Saunders enjoyed the company of her mother, sisters, brothers and aunts. She was one of twenty-five children of Nellie Orme Saunders Arnold. Her mother was married twice, the second time after her first husband was sold away to Annapolis. Although Emily's owner did not possess all in the extended Saunders-Arnold family, the family was close-knit and managed to stay in touch, even to visit. It was while visiting a sick aunt that Emily met her future husband.

Adam won the approval of Emily's owner (who did not know he was literate). In 1841, twenty-six-year-old Emily married twenty-two-year-old Adam Plummer, who was owned by Charles Benedict Calvert. Her location, however, did not change. Marriage brought motherhood to Emily, who

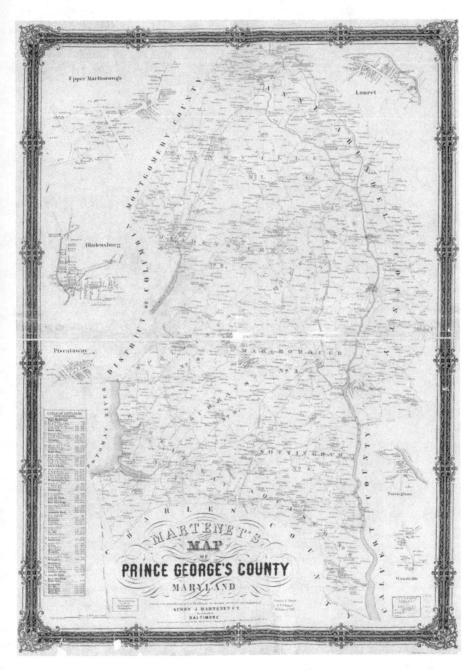

"Martenet's Map of Prince George's County, Maryland" dates from about 1861. *Library of Congress.*

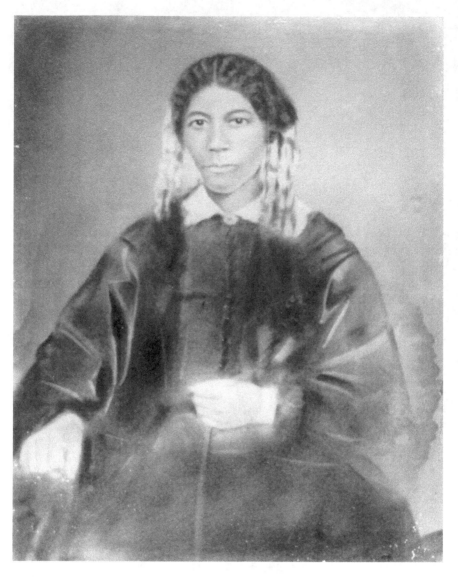

Along with her husband, Emily Plummer struggled to keep her large family together.
Anacostia Community Museum, Smithsonian Institution.

would bear nine children. With little control over her fate, it was uncertain whether Emily could raise her children in a multigenerational family as she had been.

For the first few years of marriage, Emily remained at Three Sisters with her growing brood of children. The Calvert plantation, Riversdale,

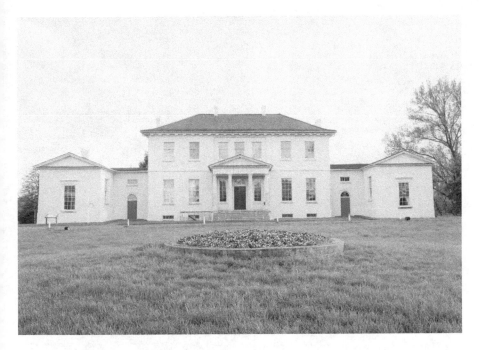

Riversdale was the home of Charles Benedict Calvert and Adam Plummer. *Cassi Hayden, M-NPPC.*

was only about eight miles away, so she could see her husband on the weekends. Adam remained fixed at Riversdale, where he continued to hold a privileged position of trust and responsibility for forty years, from slavery through Reconstruction. He had been taught literacy by an itinerant African American minister, and on Adam's visits to Emily, Adam had an opportunity to pass on his literacy quietly to some of the family. In lieu of his daily presence, when he could, Adam improved their living conditions by making furniture, fixing up the cabin and buying housewares.

The Calverts, descended from the founders of Maryland, owned and depended on Adam. Charles Benedict Calvert appreciated Adam's skills as a farmer, carpenter and shoemaker. Calvert provided Adam latitude, permitting him to keep the profits from a few acres he tilled and permitting him to take jobs for himself off the plantation in his spare time. Calvert also allowed Adam to use his skills to improve his family's living conditions even though the family members were someone else's property. Adam's owner was willing to write passes for Adam to visit his growing family. Calvert appears to have tolerated Adam's literacy because of a long history together and because of Adam's value.

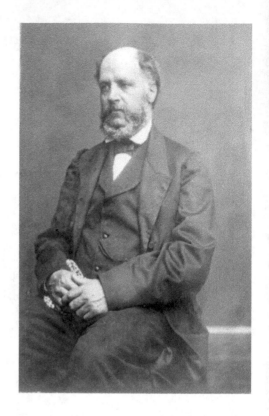

Charles Benedict Calvert came from a prominent Maryland family. *Library of Congress.*

Emily meanwhile suffered, subject to the whims of an owner and separated from her husband. Through the years as a cook and trusted family servant, Emily showed that she was responsible—except in one regard. She yearned for freedom. During Emily's years in slavery, she tried to escape more than once, but not by herself.

Emily and Adam first planned to escape to a free state or Canada in 1845, when they had only two children with whom to travel. Emily and Adam anticipated taking advantage of the unusual circumstance of their having a wedding ceremony by a white Presbyterian minister in Washington, D.C., on May 30, 1841. They had had to buy a marriage license and expected to use it in lieu of the freedom papers needed to escape detection.

Emily made a serious error by innocently trusting the extended family. She told a family member about her plans. Apparently, that family member valued her own safety or good standing in the owner's eyes over Emily's family's freedom. The betrayer handed the marriage license over to the owner when she informed her of the escape plan. The escape was aborted, and Emily was punished. She lost her status and privileges as cook and was transferred to more onerous field labor. Her sale was to come next, but the birth of her daughter Julia in 1849 postponed it. Tragically, Emily gained time at the expense of her sister Hennie, who was sold in the interim, luckily to someone within the county.

Mothers who lived in slavery feared losing their children forever through sale to "the Georgia traders," a generic term for slave traders. Especially when an owner died, enslaved mothers trembled thinking of what might happen to their children. By whim, because of debts or with cruel intent, any owner was free to dispose of his or her enslaved African Americans at any time. A will's instructions of "sale only within Maryland" were seldom honored by subsequent owners.

It was Emily's turn to tremble at the death of her owner, Sarah Ogle Hilleary, in August 1851. The terms of the Hilleary will split her possessions, including her enslaved African Americans, among her heirs. Tilman Hilleary inherited Emily and her children and was impatient to take advantage of the booming Deep South market for enslaved Marylanders. He decided to sell the Plummers. Emily's multigenerational family would be riven apart by the upcoming sale, and Emily might no longer be within walking distance of her husband. She would be torn from her lifetime home, kin and childhood friends. She would no longer have the protection of her owner, "Miss Sallie," in whose house she had worked and slept.

Emily gave birth to Saunders on October 13, 1851, and within about a week the Hillearys were advertising the upcoming sale on November 25 in the *Planter's Advocate*. Emily's owner had granted Adam the special privilege of trying to mitigate the results of sale. Adam had time enough to work out the purchase of his wife and children by a nearby couple, Mary Ann Tolley Thompson and her husband, Colonel Gilbert Livingston Thompson. This maneuver should have provided a "happy" resolution to the critical situation. It did not.

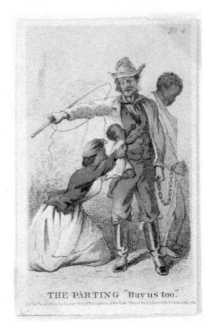

THE PARTING "Buy us too."

The Parting—Buy Us Too shows what every enslaved mother feared. *Library of Congress.*

When their turn came, Emily and her children had to suffer the humiliation of the auction block despite prior sale arrangements for at least some of them. As they stood on the block, Emily clutching baby Saunders, a trader showed interest in little Julia alone. Separation loomed. Emily could not stay quiet like a prudent bondswoman. She protested, and Julia was not sold to the trader.

That act of resistance had tragic consequences. Owner Tilman Hilleary retaliated, deciding not to include nine-year-old Sarah Miranda and five-year-old Elias after all in the sale of Emily and her children. He chose to keep them to hire out in order to provide him with a steady stream of income. That left undecided the fate of seven-year-old Henry. Then the disappointed buyer of Julia made an offer for him. Emily feared he might go to this man who boasted of being a breaker of enslaved mothers' hearts.

Her daughter Nellie would later explain in *Out of the Depths* that Emily could not bear the idea of the suffering such a sale would bring. The thought of killing herself and Henry entered Emily's mind. Death seemed better than separation or a cruel master. Temporarily, she improvised the strategy of hiding Henry in a cornfield and making him promise to stay until only

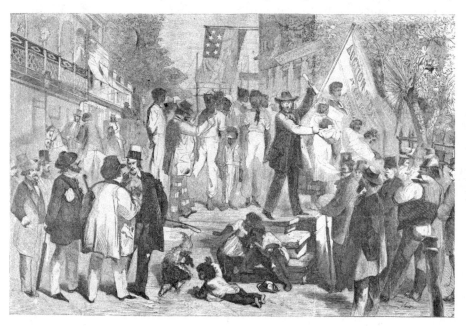

"Slave Auction at the South," *Harper's Weekly*, July 13, 1861, depicts an event occurring regularly in the District of Columbia. *Library of Congress.*

she came to get him. She had already hidden Henry in a neighbor's field when Adam arrived from packing up their possessions. He was eager to give Emily and Henry the joyous news of Henry's added inclusion in the sale to the Thompsons.

Panic quickly displaced happiness when Henry seemed to have disappeared. Adam could not retrieve Henry from his hiding place despite calling and searching. As Nellie told it, Henry's parents feared the worst, thinking he had been found by someone else and carried away for sale. If that were true, Emily had been right to despair. Beside herself, Emily rushed to find him. It was only then that he emerged from the corn shock; ironically, he had been faithfully following her orders.

On Thanksgiving Day 1851, the Plummers were together for the last time until after the Civil War. Sale was a special shock to Emily, who had lived at Three Sisters for thirty-six years with her natal family and ten years of weekly conjugal visits. After the sale, Elias stayed at Three Sisters with his aunts and grandmother. Eldest daughter Sarah Miranda was to be hired out. Emily and the rest of the children went to the Thompsons, who lived at Meridian Hill in Washington, D.C. Happily for the family, in 1852, Mrs. Thompson made an arrangement to hire Sarah Miranda; this continued for several years. Adam remained the pivotal point of the family. Meridian Hill was a possible walk for Adam every weekend or two, and he could see or hear from Emily's family members at Three Sisters if they did not visit her.

At Meridian Hill, it seemed that Emily could not relax her fears of further separation. Perhaps the death of a baby born there in 1853 increased her anxiety. Permanent separation from her children seemed to hang like a cloud over Emily's head. At nine, Sarah Miranda had now been considered old enough to earn a wage away from her mother at Meridian Hill, where she had previously been hired out from Three Sisters. Happily, the new employer, Reverend Samuel Clark, lived in Georgetown at Pilgrim's Rest, so Sarah Miranda could live with her grandmother, who had moved to Georgetown. They were near her mother and younger siblings for as long as that part of the family was living at Meridian Hill.

In 1855, Emily and her younger children moved with the Thompsons to Mount Hebron in Ellicott Mills [Ellicott City], near Baltimore. Instead of visits every two weeks, the move to Mount Hebron restricted Adam to Easter and Christmas visits to Emily and the younger children. Excluded from such reunions were their eldest daughter, Sarah Miranda, who worked at Pilgrim's Rest in Georgetown, and their son Elias at Three Sisters. It would take a mischance like Adam's serious injury in 1859 to permit Emily to visit Adam for two weeks, during which she was able to go to see Sarah Miranda. Her attempted visit to Elias failed because of the Hillearys' fears that it would impel him to escape.

The colonel was not an easy master. In order for the children to avoid his kicks and swearing, Emily had to send them running. When Colonel Thompson struck and gashed Julia, Emily had to speak up. Nellie described the confrontation that ensued in 1855. Thompson was not going to stand for what he labelled impudent behavior. He called for the constable to come to beat Emily. After the constable arrived equipped with a cowhide whip and rope, Thompson went to grab Emily. To fend Thompson off, Emily attacked Thompson with an unlikely weapon—a goose she was plucking. She then rushed to her room. Next, she made Thompson and the constable retreat by wildly threatening them with a chair. However, when Thompson's wife, Mary Ann, arrived on the scene, she had learned how to subdue Emily. Tapping into Emily's deepest fears, Mary Ann threatened sale. Mary Ann's sisters intervened. They sent for Adam to bring Emily to her senses. In the eyes of Mary Ann's sisters, Emily was too valuable to sell, outweighing Emily's resistance to Mary Ann's husband and the constable. Emily and her children continued living with the Thompsons. Nellie would triumphantly write that Emily was never whipped afterward, although other "servants" were.

Throughout the pain of slavery and separation, Emily and Adam were bolstered over the years by a strong faith in God, their love for one another and their children and the possibility of staying in contact. The Plummers found a means to deliver letters and to keep up on family news, which passed through a network of friends, family and willing whites.

Periodically, Adam was able to send Emily letters; she would get someone to read them and reply. The two reported to each other on their health, very important for a bondsperson who was always expected to be able to work. They might avoid any hint of complaint from white eyes, but in the letters, Emily could suggest the pain of separation. The letter of July 1856 read, "I cannot think that we are parted for life." In April 1859, Adam poignantly wrote to Emily of what the communication meant to him in overcoming their separation: "In the moning I wish I could see you in my haearte and in a few minnutes after a littel boy came runing to me at my House with a Letter."

Letters were not always carriers of good news. In 1857, tragedy was added onto tragedy. The Hillearys sent Emily's mother and three sisters to Levi Hurdle's slave pen in Alexandria, Virginia, a major slave-trading hub. The family members were to be sold, and two other sisters of Emily's who set out to say goodbye to their mother froze to death in a snowstorm. Adam sent the news to Emily in a letter that Mary Ann Thompson read to her. Not surprisingly, Emily reacted with violent weeping and grieving. Unsympathetic, Mary Ann said she would never read her a letter again. Following an angry retort from Emily, Mary Ann returned to threatening sale and separation. Emily's cooking, reliability and trustworthiness saved her. To protect herself, Emily found a friendly white seamstress as an alternate letter reader and writer.

Adam always included news of Sarah Miranda and Elias. Sarah Miranda is "well today and love to all of her bothers [sic] and sisters" (January 1858). Elias "is well about a week [ago] for I go to see him." (April 1859). He also included more difficult moments. Adam, in despair at the possible sale of Elias, wrote (March 1858): "sorrows encampass me Round and Endless Distresses [sic] I see astonished I cry can a mortal be found thats surrounded with troubles like me a few Hours of peace I enjoy and they are succeeded by pain."

On May 11, 1860, Adam wrote that all seemed to be well with Sarah Miranda in Georgetown. It was not. Events like John Brown's Raid on the arsenal at Harpers Ferry in 1859 and Abraham Lincoln's election as president frightened white owners. Since the 1850s, the Hillearys had been selling their bondsmen—including Emily's family—at top dollar. In her will, Sarah Ogle Hilleary had left Sarah Miranda to an heir with a guardian. The death of the guardian precipitated Sarah Miranda's sale, because Washington Hilleary took over.

In September 1860, Emily wrote her husband of "merandys trubles"— she knew in what danger her daughter lay. She was helpless, especially as she was pregnant and gave birth to twins later in the month. Along with her grandmother, Sarah Miranda tried to come visit her mother and the new babies, but she never made it, lacking a proper pass. Soon after, in September, Sarah Miranda was sent from Pilgrim's Rest, where she worked for Reverend Samuel Clark, to a slave market in Upper Marlboro, a town in Prince George's County. The infamous slave dealer B.O. Shekells bought her there and took her to the same slave pen of Levi Hurdle in Alexandria where her grandmother and aunts had been imprisoned. Sarah Miranda spent two months there until sold to Hanson Kelley of New Orleans. Reverend Clark futilely did all he could on her daughter's behalf, according to his letters to Emily. He wrote a flattering recommendation for Sarah Miranda and warned the family of potential purchasers. Nellie wrote in her book that Sarah Miranda's sale left Emily heartbroken and wishing to die. Only a vow

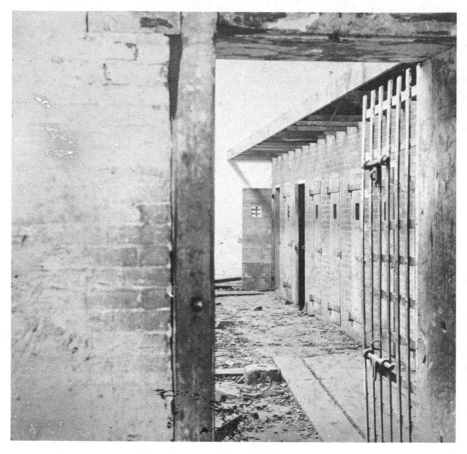

Slave traders used Alexandria, Virginia slave jails before 1861. Brady & Co. *Library of Congress.*

by Henry to find his sister encouraged Emily sufficiently to continue. Emily's grief for her eldest outweighed her love for her newborns. Emily would continue in anguish until reunited with her daughter after the Civil War.

Silence. Then a chilling letter dated May 24, 1861, came to Emily from New Orleans. Wrenchingly, Sarah Miranda wrote, "Though I may hear from you, yet I may never expect to see you again." Emily's nightmare had come true. A child had been sold far away.

It was a hard and possibly permanent separation for Emily and her family to endure. Over the years, Emily had kept escape in mind. After Congress passed the D.C. Emancipation Act in April 1862 ending slavery there, bondsmen were hopeful. Emily encouraged Henry (by now grown) to escape from the Thompsons in Maryland. This encouragement was at her own expense, as Henry had been her prop during the Thompson years without Adam at her side. Henry's accomplices were family. He hid at Riversdale with his father and then with his mother's sister in D.C. before joining the Union navy in April 1864. Though younger, Elias also escaped in May 1863.

January 1863 was a moment of jubilee for all in bondage. The Emancipation Proclamation, however, did not apply to slaveholding states still part of the Union, such as Maryland. It was a personal moment of would-be achievement of freedom. Emily tried but failed to escape. In October 1863, she fled, taking with her all five young children, ranging in age from twin babies to age fourteen. Although without a guide, they passed twice through Union soldiers and successfully traveled about fifteen miles on the way north to Baltimore. There, however, Emily misplaced her trust. Because of her treacherous guide, their money and clothing disappeared, and they were captured. They were put in the Baltimore jail as "runaways," recorded as a group surnamed "Blumbe" and listed with an approximation of the Plummers' first names.

Emily's skills and reliability stood her in good stead. She cooked for the jailor's family, earning their goodwill and paying off her and her children's expenses while incarcerated. The jailor would eventually release her only to Adam. In the meantime, Adam had a friendly customer who saw the newspaper notice of his family's capture and let him know the family's whereabouts. When he was able to go to visit Emily in jail, Adam and Emily could contemplate contingency plans. They were, however, not the only ones to do so.

An October 1863 pair of letters written to Charles Benedict Calvert by a neighbor, Thomas Donaldson, make it obvious that both Colonel Thompson and Calvert knew about the Plummer family's jailing. The letters discussed arrangements for "the negro woman & her family." The first letter considered sale or hire to Calvert of all except the older children, who would go back to Thompson's neighborhood. The second laid out two options: hiring all out in Carroll County (in nearby Maryland), or "having them with their husband" (at Riversdale). Calvert seems to have inclined toward the latter, given the final outcome.

Thompson, the owner from whom Emily and her five children had fled, had no money for the payment of the family's living expenses he needed to claim them within the allotted sixty-day period. They were released. With Adam, they took the Baltimore & Ohio Railroad to a stop near Riversdale.

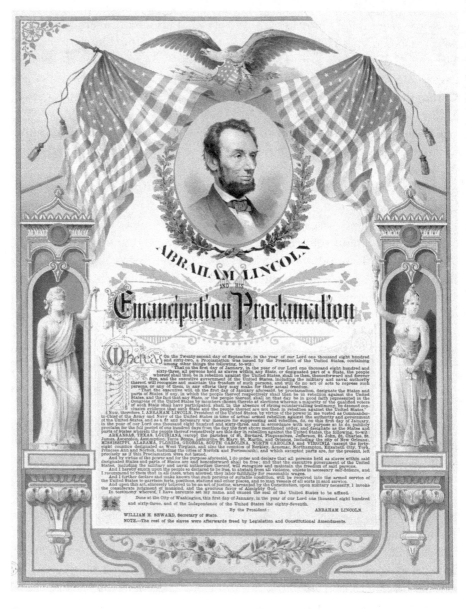

The Civil War fulfilled the promise of Lincoln's Emancipation Proclamation. *Library of Congress.*

At the plantation, Adam, Emily and five of their younger children found a permanent home together. For the next year, Emily and the children were able to live as though free at Charles Benedict Calvert's discretion. Then, Calvert's discretion was no longer necessary. The change in the state constitution in November 1864 made freedom official, as the Plummers had long desired.

Left unresolved was the threat of permanent dissolution of the family. To the relief of them all, as soon as Emily and Adam could borrow and save enough money, in 1866, they sent Henry (returned from the navy) to bring Sarah Miranda back from New Orleans. He fulfilled his vow to his mother, to the family's joy. Thanks to his sister's letters, he could locate her, although the family did not know that she had married, been widowed by smallpox and had given birth to a son. They were overjoyed at his return with his sister. That evening, they held a prayer meeting in thanksgiving. As one of the lucky formerly enslaved families, they were reunited after the Civil War.

Despite what Nellie called her mother's seven "crosses," Emily endured until freedom came and she saw her daughter again. Emily had survived physical and emotional suffering caused by: separation from her friends and kin; sale farther south of her mother, sisters and daughter; death of her sisters in a snowstorm; dread of her children's sale; mistreatment of her children by Colonel Thompson; loneliness after Henry's flight; and jail in Baltimore. It was love and faith that had enabled her and her family to continue. Nellie's commentary on the saga up through her sister's return from Louisiana was a fitting summary. She wrote, "The whole family was by the *miraculous* 'Grace of God' united under the banner of Freedom."

5

SHORT PROFILES

T he heroes in the prior chapters were not the only enslaved African Americans who resisted slavery through flight. There were many more in the D.C. area about whom we know little or nothing. To give a sense of the breadth of escapes, brief sketches are included here of individuals from various counties, about whom current research has yielded only tempting nuggets of information. The earliest sketch is of Billy, who sought freedom during the American Revolution. The latest included is about Maria Toliver, who was a refugee from slavery during the Civil War. What all in these sketches and the rest of the book have in common is a desire to act upon their hatred of slavery and love of freedom by participating in or aiding flight.

BILLY: PRINCE WILLIAM COUNTY OR DEATH

Despite the sentiments that Thomas Jefferson expressed in the Declaration of Independence, in colonial America, all men were not created equal. Before the U.S. Supreme Court's Dred Scott decision in 1857 blasted the hopes of descendants of Africans brought to the United States, there was Billy's case in 1781 in Virginia.

In Chief Justice Roger Taney's words, the Supreme Court declared in the Dred Scott decision that African Americans could not be citizens and

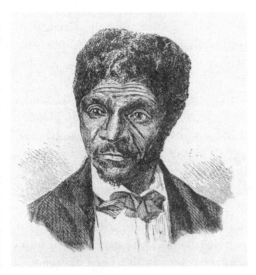

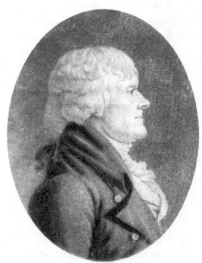

Left: Dred Scott was the subject of a Supreme Court decision that disheartened African Americans and abolitionists alike. *Library of Congress.*

Right: Governor Thomas Jefferson ultimately accepted the legal argument that a bondsman could neither be a citizen nor a traitor. *Library of Congress.*

were inferior to the extent that they "had no rights which the white man was bound to respect; and that the negro might justly and lawfully be reduced to slavery for his benefit." Decades earlier, Billy's sentence in a Prince William County, Virginia court declared bondsmen to be incapable of the duties or even the patriotism of a citizen. As a bondsman, the legal argument went, Billy (aka William, aka Will), a mulatto (light colored and of mixed race) bondsman, was a noncitizen who could not be considered guilty of treason. He was saved from death by hanging, first temporarily by Virginia governor Thomas Jefferson (1779–81), and then by permanent reprieve by the General Assembly of Virginia in Williamsburg (1781). The pardon came perhaps because Billy was a valuable property claimed by the judges to be worth an incredible 27,000 pounds. He belonged to Colonel John Tayloe, the wealthy owner of the Neabsco Ironworks in Prince William County. The ironworks employed more than 170 enslaved workers and consisted of almost twenty thousand acres of land.

Billy was tried for treason for allegedly planning to fight alongside the British navy. Lord Dunmore, the royal governor of Virginia before and during the American Revolution, had struck terror into disloyal American colonists by creating an "internal enemy." He issued a proclamation in

November 1775 offering freedom to indentured servants or Africans or African Americans willing to join the British forces. Whether or not Billy actually took the bait and ran to the British for freedom, thousands of other bondsmen did.

In Billy's defense, he claimed that he was forced on board the enemy ship and never took up arms or assisted the enemy voluntarily. He pleaded not guilty. Nonetheless, on May 8, 1781, by majority vote, the justices of Prince William County Court of Oyer & Terminer (which heard treasons, felonies and misdemeanors) found him guilty and sentenced him to be hung till dead. As a grisly public lesson, his head was to be placed on a pole at a public crossroads.

It is ironic that the author of the Declaration of Independence was in the position of acting on the petition on Billy's behalf. The decision fell upon the shoulders of a man who was adversely affected by Lord Dunmore's proclamation and who suffered moral qualms over the issue of slavery. Jefferson was not able to recover all thirty of the enslaved men, women and children from his plantations who escaped to the British. Over the years, although he deplored slavery as a "hideous blot" and a "moral depravity," he considered those descended from Africans to be childlike and inferior. With a large investment in enslaved labor, he and his planter society depended on the products of their bondsmen's work. The Billy trial demonstrated the strange logic of slaveholders. Those they dismissed as noncitizens incapable of treason were meanwhile becoming a threat to the success of the American Revolution or even the good night's sleep of its white citizens.

MARK CAESAR AND BILL WHEELER: RUNNING ON ROCKVILLE PIKE

Rockville Pike is today a busy highway passing through Montgomery County. It is hard to imagine that it was the site of a parade of armed bondsmen seen by terrified whites as an insurrection. In 1845, however, Mark Caesar and Bill Wheeler were tried for being leaders of such a march. They were coming from southern Maryland. The group had grown along the way through Maryland's Charles and Prince George's Counties to at least fifty to seventy-five followers.

The "insurrectionists" were stopped near Rockville. Pursuers managed to catch thirty-one of them, but the others reached Maryland's Carroll County, bordering freedom in Pennsylvania. Trial records have disappeared, but the Maryland Penitentiary Prisoners Record (1850) includes a law to provide a life sentence for Wheeler if he were not executed.

From biased newspaper accounts, it is hard to know if the marchers' intention was revolt or escape to freedom. After the fact, whites treated the march as a revolt and took appropriate precautions. The *Maryland Journal* of Rockville, on July 9, 1845, described the group as "seen within two miles of the place [Rockville] on the Frederick road, making their way northward in great haste." The article, perhaps inflammatory, stated that the freedom seekers were armed with pistols, bludgeons, scythe blades, swords, clubs and butcher knives. Caesar was said to be at the head, "a powerful Negro fellow, sword in hand."

A specially formed group, the Montgomery Volunteers, as well as others, succeeded in surrounding the marchers to make an attack. The freedom seekers' leader exhorted his followers to defend themselves. Nonetheless, the pursuers were able to capture thirty-one farther north near Gaithersburg (Montgomery County), wounding some of the marchers in the process. Those captured had their weapons confiscated and were taken, even if badly

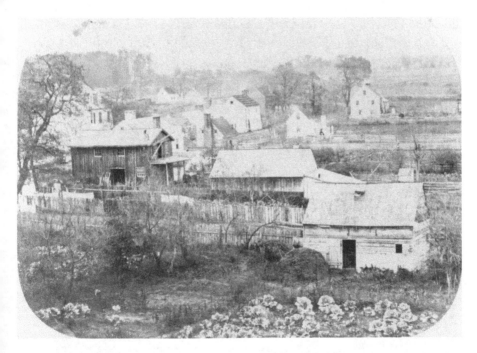

This early Rockville view was photographed after 1870. *Peerless Rockville.*

wounded, to the Rockville jail as "runaway slaves." All who had been caught were tried at the courthouse in Port Tobacco, Charles County. Over the following months, the fate for most marchers was sale to slave traders who took advantage of the incident. Some of the marchers had almost made their goal—a free state. They had evaded the pursuers and almost reached the Pennsylvania border.

In the early fall of 1845, the leaders were tried at Port Tobacco Courthouse, Caesar three days after Wheeler. Caesar, thirty-five, was easily distinguished from Wheeler, as he was literate and had a pistol ball scar on his neck. The men's indictments were separate; the probable punishment for each was death. Caesar's attorney George Brent must have been more than competent, as Caesar's jury deliberated for twenty-four hours without reaching an agreement. The new grand jury was out for blood, as it found thirty-six counts against the free man, who was guilty of "aiding and abetting slaves in making their escape from their masters." Convicted on the ten counts for which he was tried, Caesar ended up with a forty-year penitentiary sentence on November 1, 1845. He had served only until November 1850 before dying of tuberculosis.

The other leader, Bill Wheeler, initially succeeded in evading seizure but did come to trial in Port Tobacco in September 1845. His sentence to death was appealed, to no avail. The offer of a reward of $100 tells the story that, again elusive, he escaped jail in Port Tobacco in March 1846.

HORTENSE PROUT: AMONG THE MILITARY IN D.C.

In the *Washington Evening Star* of June 17, 1861, the following extraordinary article appeared:

> **A FUGITIVE**—*A slave woman belonging to Mr. John Little having eloped, Mr. Little made diligent search and ascertained that she was in one of the Ohio camps. He made visit to the camp and told the colonel commanding what he wanted, and the reply was, "You shall have her, if she is here." Search was made and the fugitive was found, completely rigged out in male attire. She was immediately turned over to the custody of Mr. Little, and was taken to jail. Every opportunity is afforded loyal citizens of loyal States to recover their fugitive slaves.*

The article was extraordinary, not for the account of the escape to the Union army or the indignation felt by the proslavery majority, but for the clever disguise. Despite desperation, a female freedom seeker was not expected to dress as a man, especially a soldier.

The daring woman was Hortense Prout. Her identity was revealed by city jail records dated June 15, 1861. These records show the committal of a woman named "Hortence" who was released on June 25 to John Little. Presumably, the newspaper had delayed printing the article quoted above.

Hortense Prout was one of John Little's eleven bondsmen living with him on his cattle farm and butchery in what was then rural Washington County, part of D.C. He had procured her parents, older sister and brother from William H. Williams and B.O. Shekell, D.C. slave traders. Little had made a profitable investment, as Hortense's mother, Delilah, and sisters Tabitha and Kalisti proved to be fertile, enriching Little by producing children who inherited their mothers' enslaved status. The Prout women worked as servants in the manor house. When Little became guardian of his niece, the total of enslaved African Americans including hers rose to seventeen. By

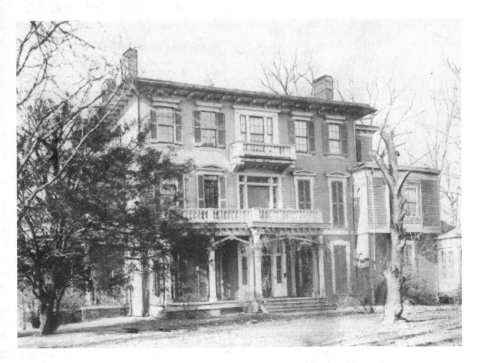

The John Little House no longer stands, but the grounds and a wayside are located at Kalorama Park, Kalorama Road and Nineteenth Street NW, Washington, D.C . *Historical Society of Washington, DC, General Photograph Collection.*

1860, Little had $40,000 in real estate and $17,000 in personal property. He had become a rich man and a seller and buyer of bondsmen. He was accustomed to lodging them in the city jail when it was convenient for him.

Only two miles away was Bloomingdale, where Ohio troops, the First and Second Regiments under A.D. McCook, had camped in May 1861 awaiting orders. They were conveniently placed near major roads leading north and northeast, that is, roads now called North Capitol Street and Bladensburg Road. It is quite possible that Hortense escaped Little on her own initiative, given how close the troops were camped and how often Union troops gave refuge to fleeing bondsmen. Perhaps no coincidence, however, there was a neighbor of Little's who was bound to be sympathetic to Hortense's plight. Jonathan Seaver was from Massachusetts and a member of the antislavery religious group the Quakers. Not only did he have free African Americans in his household, but he also had certified the freedom of several African Americans and was trustee of the Quaker burial ground right by Little's farm.

In 1862, when Hortense received her freedom, it was not through escape but under D.C.'s Emancipation Act. After swearing loyalty to the Union, John Little was compensated by the federal government for all his emancipated bondsmen, including six members of the Prout family. Hortense is listed as age twenty-one, child of Delilah, black and "a healthy and industrious house servant" for whom Little received $525.60. Subsequent censuses do not mention Hortense Prout or her sisters.

MARIA BEAR TOLIVER:
REFUGEE FROM SLAVERY IN D.C.

Refugees from slavery who arrived in Washington during the Civil War were called "contrabands." The term came from Union General Benjamin Butler's decision at Fort Monroe (May 1861) to confiscate fleeing bondsmen who had worked for the enemy as enemy "property." There was much discussion at the time of contrabands being dependent and helpless, and thus costly to care for. Maria Toliver did not fit the stereotype of the refugee women, sick or with children, who received food, clothes and patronizing advice from freedmen's aid workers like Harriet Jacob and Elizabeth Keckley. Maria Toliver is an example of a refugee who found a responsible occupation in a hospital, despite discrimination against her race

Maria Bear (later Toliver) was born in slavery about 1840 in Williamsburg, Virginia, and was later sold to someone in King William County. She took initiative and escaped about 1862. In Washington, Maria Toliver became sick and entered the "Contraband Hospital" at Camp Barker, a camp for African American refugees on R Street between Twelfth and Thirteenth Streets NW. When she recovered, only three months after her arrival in D.C., she found a job in the same hospital with Dr. James Pettigrew. Both she and her husband were nurses. She was in charge of a ward's female patients and he the male patients. She worked first in the "General" Hospital for African Americans and then the Smallpox Hospital, where her infectious patients were both African American and white. Given racism, she must have been "remarkable" in the abilities she showed and in her quickly assessing and taking advantage of an opportunity to perform work better than the menial labor of most of her peers.

PART II

IMPACT OF PLACES AND EVENTS

6

MRS. SPRIGG'S BOARDINGHOUSE

"Abolition House"

C onveniently located across from the Capitol on First Street SE, on the site of one of the present-day Library of Congress buildings, was a row of houses called first Carroll's Row and later Duff Green's Row. It consisted of six big Georgian houses made of brick. Starting about 1839, one of the buildings was the site of a boardinghouse run by a widow, Ann Sprigg.

Ann Thornton had been married to Benjamin Sprigg, who was from Virginia like she was. In Washington, her husband became a clerk in the House's Office of the Clerk. Ann Sprigg was an experienced boardinghouse keeper, as she had run an earlier establishment with four rooms on New Jersey Avenue. Sprigg had had to seek a respectable but profitable living open to women after her husband died, leaving her with three children and a fourth on the way. After his death, the congressional link would continue, with congressmen filling the boardinghouse and with their son William Bowie Sprigg's appointment as a House page.

In the 1840s, Mrs. Sprigg's boardinghouse became known as "Abolition House" because, among others, abolitionist lobbyists Theodore Weld and Joshua Leavitt boarded there. The congressmen boarding there included the allies of John Quincy Adams—Seth Gates from New York, William Slade from Vermont and Joshua Giddings from Ohio—who were the most radical of the antislavery congressmen and a small minority among the Whigs in Congress. Not coincidentally, the boardinghouse became the location of strange disappearances. Three hired bondsmen disappeared to seek freedom; a fourth, kidnapped and sold south, was rescued and returned to freedom.

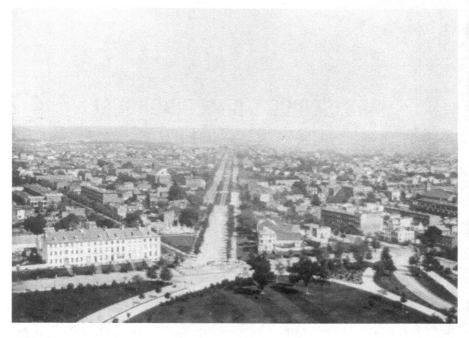

Carroll Row (Duff Green's Row) at First and A Streets SE, was built about 1800, and levelled in 1887 to make way for a Library of Congress building. *Library of Congress.*

The complicity of Ann Sprigg in the escapes is debatable, but at least a couple of her boarders were in on the secret of the escapes. One of the same boarders was also responsible for bringing the kidnapped waiter back to freedom. These incidents show how fuzzy the line could be between someone immersed in the world of antislavery politics and someone who was an Underground Railroad ally.

Boardinghouses on Capitol Hill were essential to those coming to D.C. for the seasonal sessions of Congress if they could not afford the hotels on Pennsylvania Avenue or their own establishments. Sometimes, a congressman like Abraham Lincoln brought his family with him, but most could not afford to do so. A congressman who was content with his lodging might stay ten years in the same place, as Joshua Giddings did. A boardinghouse was a place to receive visitors and mail. It was common to choose a boardinghouse where the congressman could live with like-minded or congenial colleagues. Together, they would eat and work. Historian Kenneth Winkle has compared these arrangements to a fraternity.

The unifying factor at the boardinghouses was the meals together. Such meals created a civility among people from different parts of the country.

When all sat down together to eat, they could discuss topics of the day and, of course, politics. If deeply religious, they could pray together; for some, their evangelical faith was the root of their antislavery beliefs. Enduring friendships were formed and ideas passed on. Even as the political range of boarders at Mrs. Sprigg's widened by the time Lincoln arrived in the late 1840s, there was still a comfortable togetherness. Civility moderated the heat of possible disagreements. At the table, all could laugh together; the physician Dr. Samuel Busey, who took his meals at Mrs. Sprigg's, remembered how Lincoln might interject a joke to dissipate tensions. Along with other new faces, the Lincolns had come to live at Mrs. Sprigg's in 1847–48.

In Mary Lincoln's words, Ann Thornton Sprigg was an "estimable lady," presumably because of her skills running the boardinghouse. Mrs. Sprigg's boardinghouse was set up comfortably. She could accommodate as many as twenty-five boarders, as well as building owner Duff Green and his family, who came for meals. Theodore Weld reassured his wife in a letter on January 1, 1842, that he had a comfortable bed, a dresser, desk, chairs, closets and clothes press, along with a well-supplied fireplace. Despite requiring a special diet, Weld found the food served ample and tasty. For eight dollars, Weld had room and board, light and fire, shoe brushing and what he lumped in "etc." In a letter of December 9, 1843, Abraham McIlvaine wrote home that "Mrs. Sprigg appears to be a very nice housekeeper, sets a very good table, in short

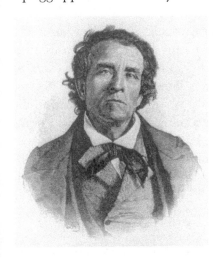

The antislavery lobbyist Theodore Weld conducted research to undermine the Gag Rule. *Library of Congress.*

we have everything necessary to make us comfortable [illegible] *except our wives and children.*" He enjoyed the "formal chat" daily after meals and visiting between neighboring rooms; his neighbor was Joshua Giddings.

In Washington in general, abolitionists and antislavery supporters were an unwelcome minority. Washington was a southern city with laws restricting African Americans. There were plenty of hard-drinking, gambling, slaveholding white citizens. Abolitionists risked being snubbed on the streets, and antislavery proponents like Adams and Giddings were threatened and insulted in the House.

Aside from the lobbyists, Joshua Giddings was the freest to express his opinions, because he came from an overwhelmingly antislavery constituency. Giddings was disgusted by slavery in D.C. and, having had a prior "spiritual transformation," was determined to act according to his conscience. He joined Adams in using opportunities, however indirect, to bring up the explosive subject of slavery in Congress. In 1842, when censured by the House for breaking the "Gag Rule," Giddings resigned; his constituency returned him to office. He called his group of antislavery congressmen a "Select Committee on Slavery." He spent his ten years at Mrs. Sprigg's boardinghouse seeing other antislavery-leaning congressmen come and go.

Ann Sprigg found that running an establishment that became known as Abolition House did not affect business. In January 1842, there were approximately twenty boarders at Mrs. Sprigg's. They were mostly congressmen, of whom eight were from Pennsylvania and the rest from other free states. In addition, there was a marine captain, a clerk in the office of the House of Representatives and a visiting lawyer. Theodore Weld, the antislavery lobbyist, rejoiced in a January 1, 1842 letter to his wife: "Only [Seth] Gates and [Joshua] Giddings [are] abolitionists, but all the others are favorable. They treat brother [Joshua] Leavitt and myself exactly as though we were not fan[a]tics, and we talk with them at the table and elsewhere just as we should at home." Courtesy shown to Weld and Leavitt meant that the gratified Weld could write, "We speak on the subject of slavery with entire freedom, nobody gainsaying us."

Sprigg's staff was a mix of African Americans and whites. Her husband, Benjamin Sprigg Sr., was a slaveholder at the time of the 1820 census, two years after he and Ann married. After his death, Ann Sprigg became a slaveholder of a curious sort. The 1840 census showed that the only African Americans in her household were free. While Weld was there, she hired or owned only bondsmen in the process of becoming free. Weld provided an explanation on December 27, 1842: "All the table waiters that were here last year have run away. Mrs. Sprigg thinks it quite unsafe to have slaves in such close contact with Abolitionists, so she has taken care to get free colored servants in their places!" On January 2, 1842, Weld noted that of the eight African Americans, "All are free but three which she hires and these are buying themselves."

Since abolition was discussed freely at the table, it is no wonder that the enslaved waiters became covetous of freedom. The waiters were surrounded by abolitionists and antislavery advocates, some of whom may have been eager to help their escape. Although they may have preferred to help with

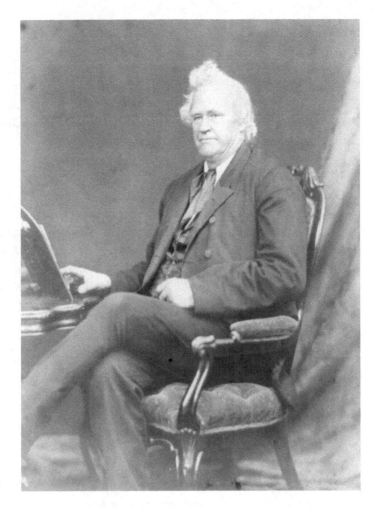

Ohio voters elected fiery Joshua Giddings as congressman. *Library of Congress.*

bondsmen's purchase of freedom, Slade, Giddings, Gates and Leavitt were all aware of the Washington, D.C. Underground Railroad activities of Reverend Charles Torrey and Thomas Smallwood.

Charles T. Torrey was a white Congregational minister from Massachusetts who had come to Washington in 1841 as a correspondent for various antislavery newspapers. Thomas Smallwood was an educated free African American from Prince George's County who eagerly managed to meet Reverend Torrey because Smallwood's wife was laundress for the keeper of Torrey's boardinghouse. The two men became partners in spiriting away bondsmen desperate to escape north. They relied on the help of Smallwood's wife, Reverend Torrey's landlady and a variety of contacts between Washington and points north. After

Torrey was apprehended, tried and imprisoned, Smallwood continued to operate the Underground Railroad alone for a year. When a freedom seeker and his host were caught in 1843, however, Smallwood had to flee with his family to Canada. Undoubtedly exaggerating, Smallwood claimed, when writing as "Samivel Weller Jr" to the editor of the *Tocsin of Liberty*, to have helped 150 people while working with Reverend Torrey between March and November 1842.

The first enslaved waiter to disappear from Mrs. Sprigg's was a mulatto man, John Douglass, hired out to Sprigg. He escaped successfully near the end of 1842. He was about twenty-three years old, six feet tall and considered by his owner to be "a first-rate house servant" who had been "a waiter in genteel families." While at Mrs. Sprigg's, Seth Gates had been sick. He was nursed by Douglass, and Douglass parlayed Gates's gratitude into a chance at freedom. When Douglass confided that his master wanted to sell him to a slave trader, Gates directed him to Reverend Torrey and Smallwood, who were organizing and conveying groups of freedom seekers north. Douglass fled, unfortunately leaving his wife and children behind. When the group grew to eighteen, the freedom seekers were ready. An operative of the Underground Railroad led Douglass's group of eighteen on foot through Maryland and Pennsylvania beyond Philadelphia. No longer as secretive, they then boldly boarded a train that took them to Canada. Douglass' brother Lewis later joined him.

In Lewis's case, one day his master came in a carriage to where Lewis worked. When Lewis spied a rope, he realized the next stop would be a slave trader's. He knew it was time to flee, so he invented the excuse of having to go to his mother's house to get the two months of wages his master wanted. There, he was in one door and out another, leaving his owner waiting in the carriage. He rushed to Smallwood, then working at the Navy Yard in D.C. Smallwood put him in contact with a friend who was butler at the house of an absent lawyer. The friend hid Lewis in the attic of the lawyer's house for three weeks until another group of freedom seekers was ready to head north. Lewis arrived safely to Canada.

The next to escape from Mrs. Sprigg's were a man Giddings referred to as "Poor Robert," who was hired out to Mrs. Sprigg for fifteen dollars a month, and another enslaved servant named Scott. In a letter to his son dated August 13, 1843, Giddings described how Robert had balked when his owner, Mrs. Harrington, set up her own boardinghouse and wanted him back. As Giddings put it, what was known next was that he was "Way up there in York State."

For six years, the antislavery group had no news of those who escaped. When no longer in Congress, Seth Gates provided an update in a December 5, 1848 letter to his friend Giddings. John Douglass had spent a night at Gates's home in New York State, during which Douglass revealed the story of his escape to Canada and told the happy ending. Douglass had returned to the United States to become a prosperous and respectable married man in Rochester. Robert and Scott had also reached Canada and also had returned to the United States. Robert was living in Buffalo by Lake Erie with his family, working as a cook on a lake steamer. Scott was also living in Buffalo.

On January 14, 1848, there was a fourth incident, this time leading an enslaved servant at Mrs. Sprigg's in the opposite direction from freedom. The kidnapping of Henry Wilson pushed the fiery congressman Giddings to overt action. Probably, it was not a coincidence that the kidnapping occurred while he was out for a walk until six in the evening. The incident at Giddings's residence indeed may have been triggered by Giddings's provocative rhetoric and behavior. After all, his thundering speeches on the House floor had made him the second-ranking antislavery advocate in Congress after John Quincy Adams, who died soon after on February 23, 1848.

At Mrs. Sprigg's, Giddings knew the remaining enslaved waiter, Henry Wilson, his free wife, Sylvia (a maid for Sprigg), and their ten-year-old son. Henry had been hired out by his owner, a widow named Mrs. Wilcoxen, to work at Mrs. Sprigg's, where he and his family lived. With the savings over and beyond what was turned over to his owner, Wilson was buying his freedom from her for $300 in installments. In happy anticipation, he and his wife had been preparing to make the final payments. Unbeknownst to them, Wilson's owner had sold him to a slave dealer, breaking the deal his owner had made with Wilson for Wilson's self-purchase.

To Wilson's surprise and his watching family's horror, the slave dealer and two assistants entered Mrs. Sprigg's and seized Wilson. Once they had thrown him to the floor, grabbed him by the throat to silence him and handcuffed him, they brandished pistols to stop resistance from anyone and rushed away with him by carriage.

Giddings returned from his walk to find Wilson's family and Sprigg grief-stricken. Giddings was able to trace the carriage to William Williams's slave pen at Seventh and Maryland SE. The pen was close, visible from the Capitol's windows. Williams, an infamous slave dealer for years, traded profitably enough that he could buy two ships to ferry his purchases monthly to the booming slave market in New Orleans. His pen not only served his own business but also served as a place to board others' bondsmen. The house's façade resembled a residence, but its backyard had a high wall and an overhanging roof to shelter purchases and boarders.

One of the other boarders at Mrs. Sprigg's was a Whig congressman named Abraham McIlvaine, who was from Chester County, Pennsylvania, a site of Underground Railroad activity. In January 1848, along with McIlvaine, Giddings proceeded to Williams's slave pen. They hoped for news of or to find Wilson.

In his *History of the Rebellion* (1864) and in a letter to the editor of the *Cleveland True Democrat* of January 24, 1848, Giddings provided enough detail to make his visit come alive. The two arrived at Williams's slave pen, called the Yellow House for its color. Its atmosphere overpowered them, aware as they were of their unpleasant errand. They braved the menacing guards and a fierce mastiff, only to be informed in a rude manner by Williams that Wilson was already on a ship headed south from Alexandria. Giddings and McIlvaine were skeptical but powerless to force Williams to change his story. They gloomily left this site of agony, despair and suffering. At its gate as they left, they encountered Sylvia Wilson, who had followed them, accompanied by some weeping relatives.

On the next day, outraged by yet another demonstration of the cruelty of slavery, Giddings reported on the kidnapping to the House of Representatives, to the disbelief of some. Details appeared in the controversial resolution by which he proposed to eliminate such incidents—his aim was to establish a committee to inquire into the end of the domestic slave trade in D.C. He intentionally provoked a divisive debate, and his resolution was voted down. He achieved his rhetorical goal but still felt obliged to help Wilson.

In his desperation, having failed with a writ of habeas corpus, Giddings turned everywhere. He tried prevailing on Mrs. Wilcoxen, but as Ezra Stevens, the Washington correspondent for the paper, put it to the *True Democrat* on February 10, 1848, "the old Jezebel was indifferent, stern, immovable in her avariciousness." So was Williams. Just when Giddings was frustrated, help came from an unexpected person, neither part of the antislavery network nor even a sympathizer.

Duff Green, the owner of the boardinghouse site, was a man of successive professions—journalist and newspaper publisher, soldier, teacher, doctor and, in D.C., a lawyer. He was as outspoken a proslavery adherent as Giddings was the reverse. Green was a slaveholder, so his motive is unknown. It may have been the violation of his property, his fear of damaging publicity for the proslavery side, his personal relationship with the man who waited on

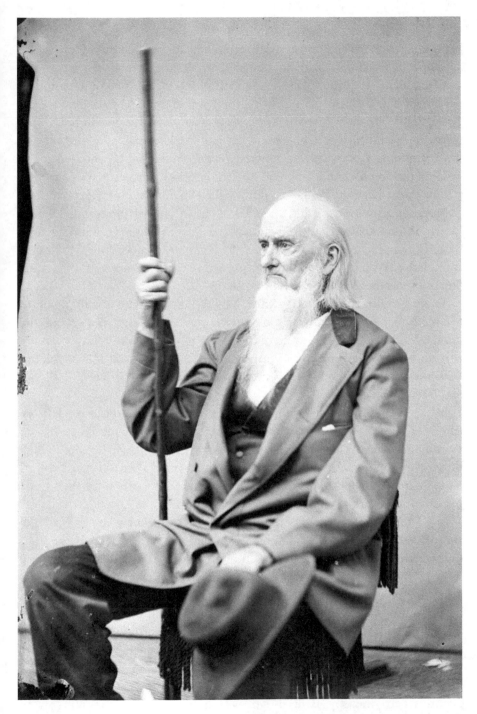

Duff Green owned the site of Mrs. Sprigg's boardinghouse. *Library of Congress.*

him daily or his sense of integrity in regard to a broken contract. Regardless, he agreed to intervene and took on the case. It was not the only case of assistance to freedom seekers that he undertook quietly.

Williams asserted that Wilson was in Richmond, up for sale by another person for $700. McIlvaine expressed the opinion to his wife on January 23, 1848, that Williams was trying for a profit above and beyond the purchase price. At the Library of Congress, there are the letters that ensued among the bargaining parties during January. After Williams had claimed to be insulted by Green's initial letter, he insisted he would negotiate only through a third party, Richard Wallach, another slaveholding lawyer. Green agreed but used pressure by asserting that "any court of any southern state" would return Wilson to freedom and by appealing to Williams's standing as a businessman. He threatened to take "efficient measures" to force Williams's compliance. Williams lowered the requested reimbursement, and the happy outcome was that Wilson was brought back.

Thanks to Green, Wilson's owner, Mrs. Wilcoxen, returned to Williams what she had received for Wilson's sale minus what she had spent of the money. Giddings and McIlvaine made up for what she had spent by a mere half an hour's collection from sympathetic members of the House. Henry Wilson was returned to his wife and young son and, by February 1848, had his "free papers."

By April 1848, Joshua Giddings had become more blatant in his actions. After the failure of seventy freedom seekers who had attempted to escape by sailing down the Potomac River on the schooner *Pearl*, he intervened. Braving a mob, he visited the ship's captains, Daniel Drayton and Edward Sayres, in jail and helped get them lawyers. It was an occasion for even more vehement speeches in Congress.

Over time, Ann Sprigg stopped keeping a boardinghouse. The 1850 census, taken in July when Congress would not have been in session, suggests that Sprigg was still taking in boarders. By 1862, the city directory showed Sprigg had moved to 392 Tenth Street West. By 1864, her economic condition was such that the Lincolns wrote a recommendation that procured her a job in the Treasury Department. She was still a clerk and living with her son when she died in December 1870. She was buried in D.C.'s Congressional Cemetery.

Meanwhile, Duff's Green was outfitted to become a Civil War prison called Carroll Prison, an annex to the Capitol Prison. It was an ill-reputed prison where the spy Belle Boyd was housed, where prisoners were detained without trial and where secret interrogations took place. For a few

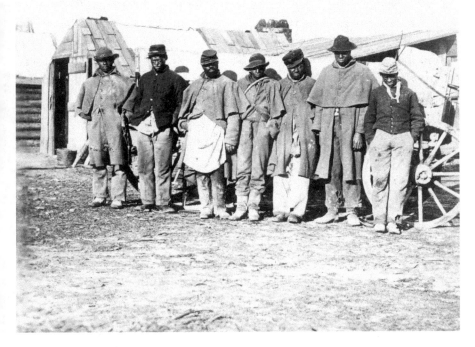

Contrabands found refuge at Union army camps. *Library of Congress.*

months while it served these purposes, part of the space housed hundreds of refugees from slavery who were drawn to D.C. after the April 1862 D.C. Emancipation Act. They were away from slavery but not yet safe from pursuers until July 1862 with passage of an act of Congress. Only a small fraction was employed and self-reliant like the earlier freedom seekers from Abolition House. Freedmen's aid worker Harriet Jacobs described the chaos and misery at Duff's Green in a moving letter to the *Liberator* of September 5, 1862: "I found men, women and children all huddled together, without any distinction or regard to age or sex....Many were sick with measles, diphtheria, scarlet and typhoid fever. Some had a few filthy rags to lie on; others had nothing but the bare floor for a couch....Each day brings its fresh additions of the hungry, naked, and sick." It took an outbreak of smallpox and the need for additional space to push those in charge to move all but those with smallpox to better conditions at nearby Camp Barker.

It is dubious to say, in comparison, that the refugees from slavery were better off than the freedom seekers from Mrs. Sprigg's boardinghouse or that the type of freedom they found was better than the limited freedom of a free African American in Washington before the Civil War. By the end of the war, through Duff Green's Row had passed people whose condition fell along a spectrum from unfreedom to freedom. While a boardinghouse, there were free whites and African Americans and enslaved and self-purchasing African Americans. As a prison and contraband camp, it sheltered not only prisoners of war but also refugees from slavery suspended in limbo, neither free nor enslaved.

7

WILLIAM CHAPLIN AND GARLAND H. WHITE

A Shared Moment

I n an Underground Railroad drama in 1850, two men—one African American, one white—from very different worlds crossed paths. By sharing minutes charged with emotion and danger, they changed the trajectories of their lives. Because their freedom mission failed, white Underground Railroad operative William Chaplin faced imprisonment and fines, and Garland H. White, a freedom seeker, narrowly escaped a death sentence—immediate in Maryland or by hard labor in the cotton South.

August 1850 was a delicate time in the District of Columbia. Congress was discussing a way to placate North and South, a discussion that would lead in September to the Compromise of 1850, including the cessation of the slave trade in D.C. to please the North and a new Fugitive Slave Act to please the South. As a result, this incident made a particular splash.

In August, the antislavery and D.C.-area newspapers were full of an attempted escape masterminded by William L. Chaplin. Police magistrate John H. Goddard and his posse of slave catchers had pounced at the D.C.-Maryland line on a carriage carrying stolen human property. Driver William Chaplin was transporting north that stolen property—two freedom seekers called "Allen" and "Garland." He was a New Yorker in Washington, a correspondent for the *Albany Patriot* who was helping African Americans desperate to escape slavery. Freedom seekers Allen and Garland belonged to Congressman Alexander Stephens and Senator Robert Toombs, respectively. The legislators, a pair of friends born in Georgia, would be prominent in the future Confederacy. Allen and Garland had already escaped from their

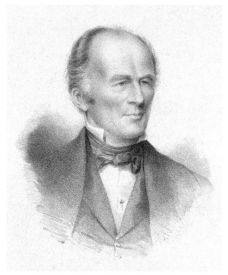 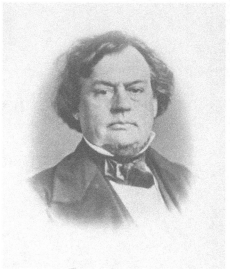

Left: William Chaplin's portrait graced the publication his sympathizers wrote and sold to raise his legal expenses. *Library of Congress.*

Right: Robert Toombs was a Georgia congressman and owner of "Garland." *Library of Congress.*

owners and been hidden among those serving General Walter Jones, a local attorney, when Chaplin tried to help them reach the Pennsylvania border on August 8, 1850.

To antislavery newspapers, Chaplin was "brave, warm-hearted, [and] sincere" and committed "a deed of mercy which would have done credit to an angel." To proslavery newspapers, he was a "negro abductor" who "seduced" the human property of slave owners and broke federal law. Chaplin himself believed he was doing his duty and following God's law in trying to alleviate suffering wrought by slavery. To the two freedom seekers, Chaplin represented the opportunity to get closer to freedom by crossing the slave state of Maryland in his carriage to reach the free state of Pennsylvania. To Underground Railroad strategists, Chaplin may have been executing a plan intended to further provoke influential southerners.

Despite nuances due to differing perspectives, the newspapers reported more or less the same story. Goddard monitored the activities of Chaplin as a known antislavery man thought to be engaged in suspicious activities. Chaplin had just returned from Pennsylvania, where he had rented a carriage that he needed to return. Coincidentally, a search was occurring for two escaped bondsmen whose owners offered an enticing $500 reward. Goddard suspected Chaplin was helping the two men. As recounted in *The Case of William L. Chaplin,* a group led by Goddard waited for Chaplin at a strategic place on the major route north, the "Montgomery Road." Goddard had prepared a posse with enough members to stop the horses drawing the carriage, immobilize the driver and make sure the passengers did not get away. As the carriage noisily and slowly climbed a hill, the posse ambushed the carriage, stopping it by locking its wheels with a rail. Chaplin, who was driving, heard shouting, then was knocked to the ground and tied up. Twenty-seven shots rang out from the weapons of the posse and the two African Americans, hitting the carriage and wounding the two bondsmen and one or more of the posse.

The posse prevailed, capturing Allen and William Chaplin. Allen was wounded, but one newspaper claimed he miraculously avoided death because of a watch he was wearing. Although also wounded, Garland fled into the woods but strangely enough returned later. He did not incriminate Chaplin but did implicate Noah Hanson, an African American man later tried for hiding bondsmen belonging to another southern congressman, William Colcock.

Chaplin and Allen were taken to the Blue Jug, the jail in Washington, and then to the city hall, which housed the courthouse. Chaplin was indicted, and the two bondsmen were returned to slavery. Chaplin maintained that he did not know the escaping bondsmen were armed and that he was merely offering them a ride north.

William Chaplin and Garland H. White could not have differed more. The "negro abductor" William Chaplin was born and educated in Massachusetts. His father was a Presbyterian minister in Groton, Massachusetts, and the family made sure William attended the best schools—Andover Academy and Harvard College. Afterward, Chaplin studied law but practiced for only a couple of years. He was drawn to the issue of the legality versus the morality of slavery. Debates after the bloody Nat Turner Rebellion in 1831 helped him to decide to devote himself to social reform. By the time he arrived in D.C. in 1844, he had been an abolitionist for fifteen years—first as an agent of the New York Antislavery Society, and then successively as editor of two antislavery newspapers, the *American Citizen* (Rochester) and the *Albany Patriot* (which had earlier employed Reverend Torrey.)

A visit to D.C. appalled him because of the slave trade and the use of federal prisons as slave prisons. As a result, he came to Washington to stay as correspondent for the Albany newspaper of which he had been editor.

He soon inherited the mantle of martyr Reverend Charles Torrey. Chaplin admired and modeled himself on Torrey but was more discreet and less provocative. Like Torrey, Chaplin attended African American churches and was known in the African American community. Like Reverend Torrey, Chaplin could not resist the African Americans who were importuning him in overwhelming numbers for advice and help.

Chaplin began by trying to purchase the relatives of those beseeching him. His admirers reported that he had raised "at least 6 thousand dollars" to help the supplicants. Nonetheless, there were instances when purchase was not feasible. Chaplin's allies Ezra Stevens and David Hall often used the courts, a process that could be long, frustrating and unsuccessful. Breaking the law by assisting flight was a last resort for Chaplin and his colleague Jacob Bigelow. Chaplin, however, soon felt himself pushed into jointly arranging the failed large-scale escape of seventy-plus bondsmen on the *Pearl* (1848) and into undertaking the politically embarrassing botched escape of Garland and Allen.

Unlike Reverend Torrey, who seemed to have fewer D.C. colleagues (only his landlady and African Americans John Bush, Thomas Smallwood and Smallwood's wife), Chaplin was much less alone in what he did. Backing Chaplin there was now what historian Stanley Harrold called a D.C. community of "subversives." At various times, Chaplin worked with white colleagues like Ezra Stevens, David Hall and Jacob Bigelow; he also worked with African American colleagues like Warner Harris, who was jailed after Chaplin's exploit, and Luke and Sarah Carter, who became operatives after receiving his help. Chaplin's letters and the campaign to raise bail for him show that he had built a biracial antislavery and abolitionist network. The network extended from D.C. to New York State and included philanthropists like Gerrit Smith, who helped fund the *Pearl* escape and Chaplin's bail. While Torrey and Smallwood's network had stretched from Delaware through Philadelphia and Albany, including fellow operatives like Jacob Gibbs (Baltimore) and James J.G. Bias (Philadelphia), it seemed more dependent on the resources of those they were assisting.

Chaplin not only acted directly but also wrote for a northern constituency. To raise money and create sympathy, he would relate cases of possible sale south. His writing was a strategy in the propaganda war waged by the small groups of antislavery activists and abolitionists. Many Northerners were unfamiliar with the South, slavery and African Americans. Like others, Chaplin emphasized what those he was helping had in common

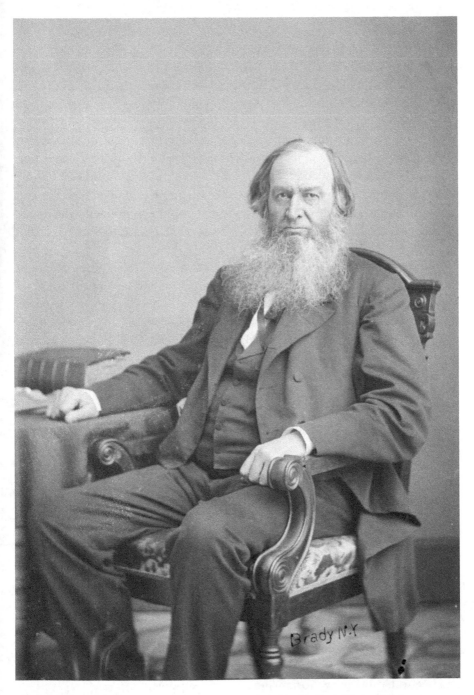

Gerrit Smith subsidized the attempted escape on the ship the *Pearl*. *Library of Congress*.

with the readers he was trying to win over. In the articles he wrote for the *Albany Patriot*, he referred to the shared work ethic and Christian morality, as well as to the horrors of slavery. The intent was that such articles might get picked up by other papers or inspire other sympathetic journalists to write about brutal punishments, sexual exploitation and the degradation of being human property.

After the arrest, Chaplin's allies rallied. Just after the arrest, on August 21, abolitionist Frederick Douglass presided over a Fugitive Slave Convention held in Cazenovia, New York. There, after a report on a visit to Chaplin by a New York friend, Joseph C. Hathaway, conventioneers hailed Chaplin as a hero and a martyr. Not only did attendees set up a committee to raise bail, but they also made plans to commission a silver pitcher inscribed to him as a testimonial.

The dramatic arrest incited supporters of slavery to demand punishment for Chaplin. He was indicted in D.C. for abduction and larceny. By the time his supporters raised the $6,000 bond for his bail and Chaplin was released from the Washington jail, the governor of Maryland had requested his transfer to Montgomery County, Maryland. There, Chaplin was charged with larceny, assisting escape and assault and battery with intent to kill. When he was indicted on the first two of these charges, the pressure from slaveholders led the judge to set an astronomical $19,000 bail.

Chaplin and his sympathizers could not help remembering the tragic fate of Reverend Torrey, Chaplin's predecessor with the D.C.-area Underground Railroad. Torrey had died of tuberculosis in 1846 in a Maryland prison after his trial and sentencing. The conditions in the jail at the county seat in Montgomery County were equally overcrowded and filthy. The sympathizers wanted Chaplin to avoid Torrey's fate. Considering Chaplin only guilty of "excessive and romantic generosity," his sympathizers published a booklet to publicize his plight and approached many antislavery supporters in order to raise money for the bail. Washington attorney David Hall, merchant Selby Parker and New York abolitionist Gerrit Smith risked their property and fortunes by contributing.

Chaplin's case was to be deferred until the following March and to be moved to Ellicott City, a venue in present-day Howard County, so he could get a fairer trial. The presiding judge there, however, was rumored to want to sentence Chaplin to the penitentiary for life. Chaplin decided to forfeit bail and flee to Upstate New York, where he had support.

After his guarantors posted his bail in Annapolis, Chaplin took the opportunity to expeditiously head north. Once there, he married his fiancée

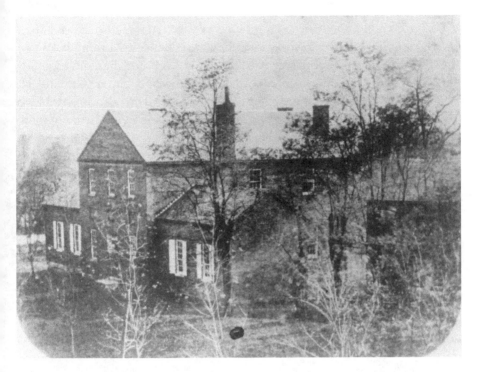

The Rockville Courthouse looked like this in the 1870s. *Peerless Rockville.*

and went on the lecture circuit in New York State to try to raise money to repay those who had posted his bail in Maryland. Ironically, two of these generous men were financially ruined by loss of the unrepaid bail money. Chaplin's African American associates were placed in jail and the freedom seekers were returned to suffer their owners' displeasure. Critics like Gerrit Smith pointed out that the large forfeited bail could have been better spent to give freedom to other desperate bondsmen or to otherwise further the antislavery cause.

After 1851, disillusioned, Chaplin separated himself from aggressive tactics. Strain took a toll on him, and he drew back from lectures or a return to D.C. to stand trial. Instead, he, his wife, Theodosia, and his friend James C. Jackson turned to running a Glen Haven, New York water cure establishment that promoted health and dress reform. When he died in 1871, his obituary in a local paper praised him for his beneficent work in antislavery and temperance reform but omitted mention of his arrest and persecution by slaveholders. Perhaps his peers in New York considered Chaplin's Underground Railroad history to be unsavory.

Unlike Chaplin, the African Americans involved in the unsuccessful 1850 escape were left on their own to face the consequences. Nothing is known about the future of freedom seeker Allen and little about Chaplin's associate Warner Harris. The history of "Garland" is another matter. Garland H. White was an inveterate letter writer and joined the army, so it is possible to track him through service records, censuses and letters in order to compare his subsequent life to Chaplin's. Perhaps as a result of the confidence given him by his later successful escape, White went on to reach a pinnacle of success not imaginable for an enslaved African American.

"Garland," as he was called, had been born in Hanover County, Virginia, but while young was separated by sale from his mother. Robert Toombs, who served a long career in Congress before becoming secretary of state for the Confederacy and a brigadier general in the Confederate army, purchased Garland in Richmond. He made Garland his body servant, taking him back and forth between Georgia and Washington, D.C. At the time of the first escape of Garland, Toombs was his legal owner. Garland was on good enough terms with Toombs to continue in his service after the shoot-out rather than to be sold. Punished or not after the escape,

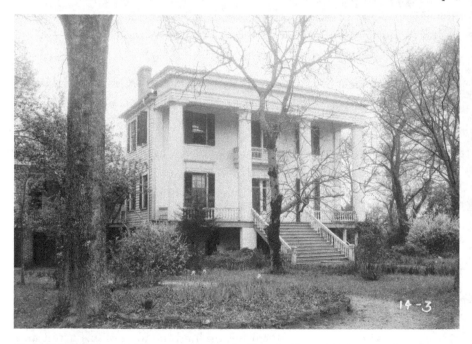

Garland H. White would have spent time at the Toombs House, Washington, Georgia, belonging to Garland White's owner. *Historic American Buildings Survey, Library of Congress.*

Garland made use of his time with Toombs to become licensed to preach the Gospel in 1859.

Toombs did not heed the near escape masterminded by Chaplin and so was not alert enough to prevent Garland's successful escape to Canada. Garland settled in London, Canada West, an area with other refugees from slavery. He married and had a daughter. He was listed on the 1861 Canadian census as a laborer, but the London Mission run by the British Methodist Church (an African Canadian denomination) appointed him a preacher. He had definitely learned to read and write by the time he reached Canada, as attested to by the 1862 letter in his Civil War pension file offering his services to Edwin Stanton, the secretary of war.

By age thirty, Garland had created a free identity in Canada. In the census of Canada West in 1861, Garland H. White appeared with the initial and surname he would use for the rest of his life. It became apparent that White was both a religious and an ambitious man. He became a persuasive speaker, progressing from enslaved preacher in Georgia to freed preacher at the London Mission, to recruiter for the U.S. Colored Troops and to chaplain in the Union army.

Evidently, Reverend White was also a persuasive writer. Despite his years in slavery, he was not afraid to launch a letter-writing campaign after his arrival in Canada. He created his own supporters rather than becoming a martyr lauded in abolitionist newspapers. He felt an allegiance to the United States, if only to his fellow African Americans, and sought the chance to destroy the hated institution of slavery. He saw an opportunity among like-thinking fellow freedom seekers in Canada. He offered his services to Secretary of War Stanton, first as a Union army recruiter in Canada on May 7, 1862, and later as a military guide in Georgia on July 29, 1864. There is no record that Stanton acted on Reverend White's

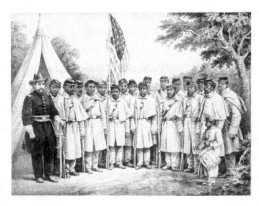

"Come and Join Us Brothers," begs this poster of the Supervisory Committee for Recruiting Colored Regiments. *New York Public Library*.

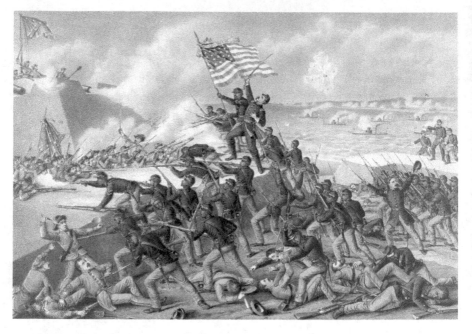

The Fifty-Fourth Massachusetts Infantry Regiment, U.S. Colored Troops, bravely stormed Fort Wagner in July 1863. *Library of Congress.*

letters, but White moved his family back to the United States to Ohio. He served a church in Toledo and plunged into recruiting. He went on to enlist men for the famous Fifty-Fourth Massachusetts Regiment U.S. Colored Troops as well as for much of the Twenty-Eighth Indiana Regiment U.S. Colored Troops. Although he himself enlisted as an ordinary soldier, his goal was to become a chaplain in the army, a rare position for an African American man to obtain.

When an enslaved servant, Reverend White had known former senator William Seward, who was secretary of state in Lincoln's cabinet by the time of White's letter of April 27, 1863. White did not hesitate to use that acquaintance to build a relationship by writing Seward repeatedly, asking for advancement in the army and for favors such as support in his campaign to become an army chaplain. He also wrote to commiserate after a near-fatal attack on Seward in April 1865.

Reverend White mounted a successful campaign to become army chaplain of the Twenty-Eighth Regiment U.S. Colored Troops—by writing letters, recruiting soldiers to complete the regiment and lobbying white regimental officers. He managed to get elected by fellow soldiers and then appointed

in September 1864. He did well enough
as chaplain to receive a tribute from his
regimental officers at his mustering out.
His letters, and the tribute from his fellow
officers and two reports of his discovered
by historian Edward Miller Jr., show how
Reverend White fulfilled his duty to create
an educated and moral Christian regiment.
He was not content to confine himself
to holding prayer meetings and services.
The materials describe his organization
of classes, conversion campaigns and
subscription to and sale of the Methodist
newspaper the *Christian Recorder*. He wrote
letters to the *Christian Recorder* on behalf of
his men and his fellow African American
soldiers, defending their bravery and
accomplishments (October 21, 1865). A

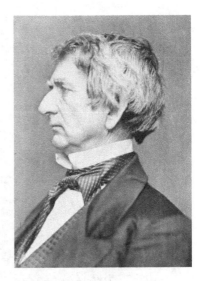

William Seward was Lincoln's
secretary of state. *Library of Congress*.

letter describing an execution (May 6, 1865) and another describing both the
regiment's triumphant arrival in Richmond and White's touching reunion
with his mother (April 22, 1865) showed the dramatic improvement in his
writing since Canada.

Miller has traced the remainder of Reverend White's life. After the
war, White returned to Toledo and then served a church in Halifax,
North Carolina. In Toledo, he prospered, acquired real estate and had
two more children. He continued as a pastor in North Carolina and D.C.
He was active in church congresses and author of a Negro Declaration
of Independence from the Republican Party issued by the National
Independent Political Union in 1876 in Washington, D.C. In the postwar
years, although he continued his religious duties, his health suffered. In his
final years, he mounted a new campaign—to obtain himself a veterans
disability pension and successive increases. He moved to Washington
and again used his networks, calling on regimental comrades to submit
the affidavits in his pension file. He was successful but had to work as a
messenger to supplement the pension. He died in 1894 and was buried in
Arlington Cemetery.

Judging by Chaplin's obituary and gravestone, the arrest in 1850 was
a moment to forget. His obituary in 1871 mentioned only his antislavery
activities in New York, and his stone lists merely his and his family's names

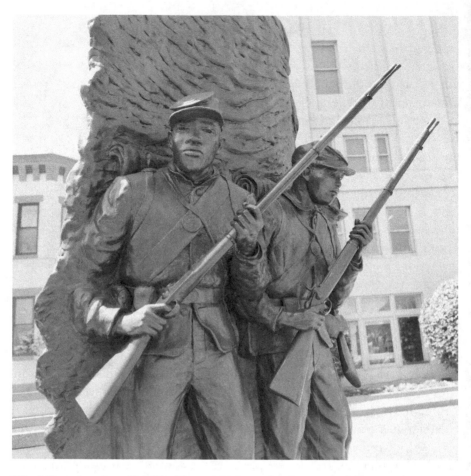

The African American Civil War Memorial is located at the corner of Vermont Avenue and Tenth and U Streets NW, Washington, D.C. *Corinne Masur.*

and dates of birth and death. The gravestone is unlike Reverend Torrey's monument in Cambridge, which celebrates his Underground Railroad career. Judging by Reverend White's letters and his burial in Arlington Cemetery, the arrest was part of a pursuit of freedom that defined the rest of his life. The freedom he achieved after his second escape shaped his subsequent life by enabling him to become chaplain for the Twenty-Eighth Indiana U.S. Colored Troops and to continue his religious career as pastor after the Civil War.

As required by the military cemetery, White's tombstone engraving had to be simple—name, company, regiment and date of death. The burial itself, though, was an honor. The letters fellow officers wrote at mustering out were merited by his Civil War service. If White had any fame, it was of his own making.

Ironically, operative William Lawrence Chaplin, who was white, followed the path of certain freedom seekers. He was jailed and, when freed, went to join the abolitionist lecture circuit. On the other hand, Reverend Garland H. White, the freedom-seeking enslaved African American, instead of receiving punishment or sale for his first escape, sought freedom a second time, this time reaching Canada. Then, ironically, when he returned to the United States to fight against slavery, he followed the trajectory of white abolitionists who became officers in the United States Colored Troops. Like the abolitionists, he successfully used literary talents and networking to further his aims.

PART III

OPERATIVES, ACCOMPLICES AND HELPERS

8

LEONARD GRIMES

He Never Forsook the Underground Railroad

In 1863, Leonard Grimes was living in Boston when his parishioner William Wells Brown described him as "above middle size, good looking" and having "a countenance which has the appearance of one who has seen no trouble." Calling his expression "untroubled" was ironic, however, given the many risks Grimes had undergone in pursuing freedom for the enslaved between the 1830s and the Civil War.

Grimes knew slavery firsthand. He was born about 1814 in Loudoun County, Virginia, near Washington, D.C. In 1826, at "about twelve years of age," he was recorded as born of free parents. When young, he had gone to work in Washington as a butcher's boy in a city market and as an apothecary's clerk, but he had the most success working with a local slaveholder. If life in Leesburg and D.C. was not a sufficient education in the horrors of slavery, he was confronted with them during this job. When Grimes traveled in North Carolina with the slaveholder, he was present at the beating of an enslaved woman who refused to leave her dying child to go work. Sickened by the sight, he left the slaveholder's employ.

Grimes used his savings to set up a business. He transported passengers in his horse-drawn taxi, one of the only occupations allowed free African Americans in D.C. by an 1831 law. With his business established, he was able to buy property at H and Twenty-Second Streets NW, to marry Octavia Colston in 1833 and to start a family. Despite the risks to himself and his family, he plunged into Underground Railroad activities. It is not known if he worked alone or had contacts to the North. Transporting customers all over D.C. and northern Virginia was a cover for Grimes's activities on the Underground Railroad—that is, until 1840.

In 1840, rumor of Grimes's collusion with the escape of a bondswoman named Patty and her children reached their owner, Joseph Mead of Loudoun County. He swore out a writ of habeas corpus in January 1840; by March, the trial against Grimes was underway in Leesburg. Grimes had fulfilled his role as Underground Railroad operative, but the decision to drive Patty and her children from Leesburg to D.C. proved disastrous for him.

Grimes's lawyers argued that the testimony against him was weak because there was no reliable witness placing him in the vicinity of the missing family either while they were enslaved or while they were escaping from Virginia. The main witness against him was an

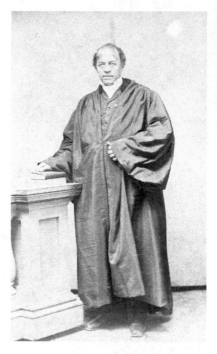

After prison, Reverend Leonard Grimes went on to continue Underground Railroad work in Boston. *Library of Congress.*

alcoholic who possibly committed perjury. The shaky testimony that sent Grimes to prison for two years was based on two grounds, neither of which had to do with proximity of the freedom seekers to Grimes or his carriage. The damning testimony was that Grimes did not stop as usual at the Hardy carriage stop on the turnpike on his way to Washington and, while passing the carriage stop, he kept his shades down, hiding the identity of his passengers.

The story Grimes admitted to years later was that a freeman, Vincent Douglass, the husband of a woman named Patty, appealed to him. Douglass's six children were enslaved because they inherited the enslaved condition of their mother. Douglass wanted his wife to escape with their children in order to join him in Canada, where she and the children could be free. Patty and her children indeed reached their destination, according to the abolitionist newspaper the *Emancipator* of December 5, 1839.

Grimes's eloquent defense attorneys included John Janney, from a local family known to be against slavery, and General Walter Jones, well known in D.C., who defended pro- and antislavery clients alike. At the trial, the defense

The indenture documents the location of Leonard Grimes's property in D.C. *Nidiffer Family Collection, Georgetown University Library, Booth Center for Special Collections.*

attorneys stressed Grimes's well-known good character and produced letters attesting to such, but he was convicted nevertheless. The case was argued before a large, rapt and volatile audience. The potential for violence may have intimidated the jury. The testimony of witnesses describing Grimes's good character did help result in what was considered a "light" sentence—

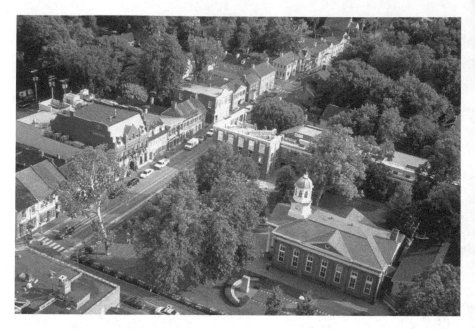

A modern aerial view shows the courthouse (with tower) in Leesburg, Virginia. *Loudoun County Economic Development, Virginia.*

two years in prison and a $100 fine he could not easily pay. He was sent to the Virginia state penitentiary in Richmond and served his full term, despite his lawyers' petitions to the governor for a pardon.

Grimes's lot was hard labor and chains. He must have grieved over separation from his friends and family and his ruined business. But, during the years of imprisonment, something else happened that would change the course of his life. He underwent a spiritual awakening, according to a friend, what he called "that great spiritual change which makes all things new for the soul." He found a divine purpose for his imprisonment and began to preach to the jailors and his fellow prisoners. Upon his release, Grimes returned to D.C. and became licensed to preach. He now pursued a dual mission—participating in the Underground Railroad and living according to his newly found faith.

After Grimes's release from prison, it was not safe for him to continue in the hack business, so he resorted to hauling furniture. He resumed responsibility for his wife and his three children, his property and the management of his debts. In the interim of imprisonment, he had left his property, family, debts and hack business in the care of his uncle William Bush. Bush, also from Loudoun County, had also moved to Washington and was active in the Second Baptist Church in D.C. It is not known if Grimes resumed Underground Railroad activities in D.C. or if Bush was also involved in the Underground Railroad, albeit more cautiously than Grimes. Neither Bush nor his wife, Lucinda, ever came to the notice of the law. Following a Bush family tradition, historian Kathryn Grover links Lucinda's participation in the attempted escape on the schooner *Pearl* to the Bushes' precipitous move from Washington to New Bedford, Massachusetts, afterward.

Even before his uncle's move, Grimes and his family had left slaveholding Washington for the free state of Massachusetts. New Bedford beckoned, as it was a whaling port with a substantial African American population and many jobs for African Americans. As an added attraction, Grimes knew Lucinda's brother, who had already come from Washington to New Bedford.

Grimes earned a living in New Bedford by taking a partner and setting up a store. He was in New Bedford when his fourth child was born in 1846. Most importantly, Grimes did not give up his religious vocation, which would fuel his antislavery convictions.

Grimes resumed open Underground Railroad participation after his move from New Bedford to Boston. He was invited to serve a small African American congregation in nearby Boston organized as the Twelfth Baptist Church in November 1848. At the time of his appointment, he was ordained. His church became the fifth in Boston's African American community and, like the others, a support to African American community life. Although Boston's many abolitionists made the city a beacon for freedom seekers, African Americans were a beleaguered minority without the full rights of white citizens. Churches provided them with a needed sphere of their own.

It was his twenty-seven years as pastor of the Twelfth Baptist Church that distinguished Reverend Grimes as a "Man of Mark" in William J. Simmons's book of that name (1891). Under Grimes's direction, Twelfth Baptist Church became a church to be reckoned with. It prospered enough to buy a lot on which to build a church with a capacity for hundreds of worshippers. Grimes became a high-profile African American minister, tied into networks of rich whites and diverse sectors of African Americans. He was in an ideal position to help refugees from slavery. Tellingly, his church became called the "Fugitive Slave Church" due to the large number of members who had fled slavery.

Passage of the Fugitive Slave Act in 1850 was a bitter blow to which Reverend Grimes reacted publicly. His congregation shrank, because the act drove an estimated forty to sixty scared Twelfth Baptist Church freedom seekers to Canada. Boston might be an antislavery stronghold, but its

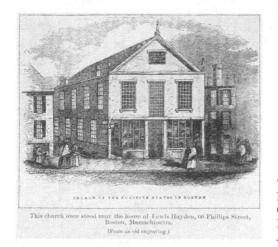

This church once stood near the house of Lewis Hayden, 66 Phillips Street, Boston, Massachusetts.
(From an old engraving.)

"Church of the Fugitive Slaves in Boston" is what many called Leonard Grimes' Twelfth Baptist Church, Boston, Massachusetts. *New York Public Library.*

residents were still subject to predations of slave owners and slave hunters. Slave catchers delighted in the Fugitive Slave Act of 1850, which reinforced and strengthened the Fugitive Slave Act of 1793. Flight was a crime in both, but the 1850 act punished accomplices more stringently and facilitated return of freedom seekers to slavery by turning over control of enforcement to the federal government.

Reverend Grimes publicly involved himself and his church in support for Boston's "first" and "last" captives arrested under the 1850 Fugitive Slave Act. Grimes participated in Shadrach Minkins's 1851 escape from court, during the first test of compliance with the law. Only four years later, in 1854, Grimes was one of the Boston residents making sure that Anthony Burns did not stay in the slavery to which the last Massachusetts test of the Fugitive Slave Act condemned him.

In February 1851, a freedom seeker named Shadrach Minkins was discovered in Boston by a pursuer from Norfolk, Virginia. Known as Frederick Wilkins or Frederick Jenkins, Minkins had lived nine months in Boston after fleeing from service to John DeBree, a navy man in Norfolk. With ready access to sailors and stevedores in the docks, Minkins had found an opportunity to escape by ship to Boston. After living some months in Boston, he was suddenly seized at his workplace, a coffeehouse in central Boston. He had been arrested by federal officers. At the ensuing hearing, Leonard Grimes was there to reassure the man who had become his parishioner. Minkins would surely have been turned over to pursuers under the Fugitive Slave Act. Only three hours after the arrest, however, a band of African American men rushed him from the courthouse to the West End of the city. At that point, their mission became a success, because Minkins disappeared, never to be recaptured. After Minkins was carried out of court by a crowd of African Americans, Grimes followed, catching up as the group neared his church. What happened next long remained a mystery, although there were rumors that Minkins reached Montreal.

Later in February, Grimes turned to dispersion of other scared freedom seekers from Boston who were in cahoots with the Boston Vigilance Committee. The committee was formed to aid and defend those fleeing slavery, and treasurer Francis Jackson noted payments to accomplices in the account book he kept. In February 1851, the Boston Vigilance Committee reimbursed Reverend Grimes for prior transportation for James Dale; Isaiah Gaiter; William Peters to Southboro; and James Harris to Halifax, Nova Scotia.

In 1854, Reverend Grimes played a more publicized role in the case of Anthony Burns. Burns had been born in bondage in Stafford County, Virginia, and hired out to work in Richmond or Falmouth. Like Minkins, he arrived at Boston hidden in a steamboat and found a job. In his exuberance,

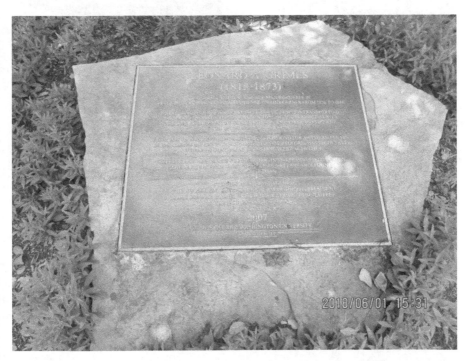

Leonard Grimes is commemorated by a plaque where his property stood at Twenty-Second and H Streets NW, on the campus of George Washington University. *Jenny Masur.*

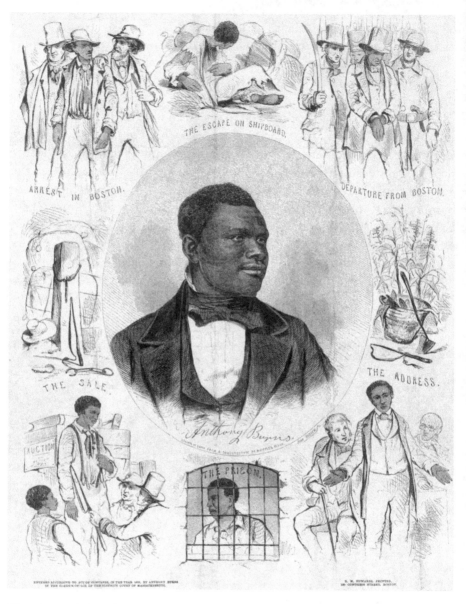

The seizure of Anthony Burns caused a ruckus in Boston. *Library of Congress.*

he sent a letter to his brother revealing his location, a letter unfortunately intercepted by Anthony's owner, Charles F. Suttle. Suttle rushed to Boston and there discovered Burns. He seized him and made sure he was jailed. Amid a flood of public controversy, the Boston Vigilance Committee engineered an unsuccessful attack on the courthouse. The result was a dead deputy federal marshal and a prolonged "rendition trial." Despite defense by renowned Boston attorneys, the outcome was the much-publicized return of Burns to slavery. Federal troops had to protect Burns from rescue by the crowds as he was put on a federal revenue ship headed south from whence he had fled.

Reverend Grimes took time from his duties as pastor to raise money from rich friends and negotiate the purchase of Burns's freedom from his new owner. After Grimes and his church raised $1,300, in 1855, Grimes took the all-important checks to the man claiming ownership.

After these fugitive slave cases, Reverend Grimes continued to work in the cause of freedom by advocating the incorporation of African American men, free or enslaved, into the Union army. Those who enlisted would attain free status by the end of the war. Grimes recruited for the Fifty-Fourth Regiment of the U.S. Colored Troops, a regiment mustered in Boston that included African Americans from far and wide. Although he was honored by being invited to be the chaplain of the Fifty-Fourth Regiment, he declined because of his duties at Twelfth Baptist Church. He lived to see the Thirteenth Amendment ending slavery all over the United States and to be able to assist the newly freed.

9

JOHN DEAN

Fighting the Fugitive Slave Act

There is a misconception among many people that the Emancipation Proclamation, issued in January 1863, brought freedom to all in slavery. It did not. The South recognized the war's cause as slavery, but Lincoln's initial goal was preserving the Union. He allowed slavery to exist in the loyal border states. Although Congress emancipated the District of Columbia's enslaved African Americans with compensation to owners in April 1862, Maryland did not revise its constitution until November 1864. Meanwhile, its bondsmen still sought refuge in D.C. In 1863, after the appointment of the first D.C. Fugitive Slave Commissioners to hear cases under the Fugitive Slave Act, at least fifty fugitive slave warrants were issued in D.C. for the arrest of bondsmen fleeing Maryland during the month of May alone.

In March 1862, lawyer John Dean arrived in Washington from New York looking for a job to pay his debts. He found more than the paying job he expected to find in the government. In less than two years, this ardent Unionist became a recognized advocate for Maryland's fleeing bondsmen. He may not always have successfully rescued the "fugitives" he defended, but he brought an important issue before the D.C. Circuit and Supreme Courts and drew national attention. He used the D.C. courts repeatedly to test the legality of the Fugitive Slave Act in D.C. and U.S. territories. In the course of his use of the courts, he came up against all components of the system enforcing the Fugitive Slave Act of 1850—the act's commissioners, the judges, the claimants of bondsmen and their attorneys and the proslavery public supporting the system. The more

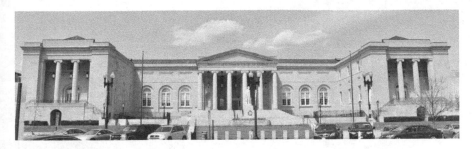

The Old D.C. City Hall at Judiciary Square served as the nineteenth-century D.C. courthouse. It is once again a courthouse. *Corinne Masur.*

freedom seekers he defended, the more emotionally as well as intellectually involved he became in their plight.

By 1862, Dean had already proven himself an antislavery man. After graduating from Hamilton College in 1832 and reading law in Utica, Dean opened a law practice in Deansville, his hometown. He moved to Brooklyn, New York, in 1851 to set up a joint practice with Judge Abraham Soper in New York City and, by 1856, was president of a local Republican group. Through the Plymouth Congregational Church in Brooklyn, he made a fateful acquaintance with antislavery activist Reverend Henry Ward Beecher. Beecher had caught national attention by preaching a sermon so eloquent that it wrung listeners' hearts and opened their purses, thereby saving two Maryland sisters on the verge of sale farther south.

Dean's Brooklyn law practice prospered until the financial crisis of 1857 and his near-fatal illness in 1860. With a wife and six children, he was desperate to both pay his debts and support his family appropriately. By August 1861, Dean was corresponding about possible work in D.C. with John Curtis Underwood, the fifth auditor of the Treasury Department. Underwood was a fellow New Yorker, a classmate from Hamilton College and enough of an advocate against slavery that he had had to leave Virginia. Underwood had been part of two schemes to demonstrate the viability of free labor in Virginia, in addition to participating in the fledgling Virginia Republican Party.

Upon arrival in D.C. in mid-March 1862, Dean immediately called upon Underwood. Dean hoped for a Treasury position, because Underwood was well connected to Secretary of the Treasury Salmon Chase. Chase, a former governor of Ohio, was himself well known for defending Margaret Garner, who had preferred to murder her children in 1856 rather than allow their return to slavery.

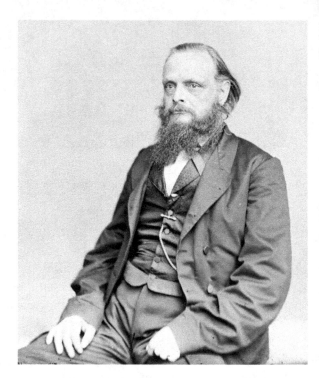

John C. Underwood
worked in the Department
of the Treasury until
appointed a judge in
Virginia. *Library of Congress.*

In D.C., Dean wrote his wife that he found "many friends from New York" beside Underwood. Dean quickly made himself useful, visiting New Yorkers in military hospitals when he was not networking to find a job or delivering letters of recommendation. Further, Dean acquainted himself with Washington and the situation of African Americans. For firsthand information, he interviewed both slaveowners and those refugees from slavery called "contrabands." He visited the contraband camp at Duff's Green and attended meetings of the National Freedman's Relief Association to better understand the refugees' situation. He brought himself up-to-date on emancipation by going to the Capitol to hear Senators Charles Sumner, the radical Republican from Massachusetts, and Garrett Davis, the Unionist from Kentucky, speak. Dean's "respectable colored waiter" from his lodgings recognized his connections by asking Dean to serve as liaison for an African American community concert in homage to advocates of emancipation. A clipping in Dean's papers makes it obvious that he was aware of Seward's 1861 order preventing the army from returning any Virginia freedom seekers to slavery.

Before Congress had a chance to pass the D.C. Emancipation Act of April 15, 1862, Dean published an article in the antislavery newspaper the *National Republican* on April 10, 1862. It was called "Slavery in Its Dying Agonies,"

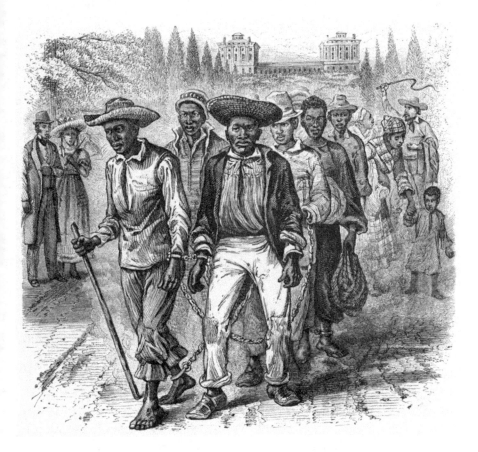

A slave coffle passes by the U.S. Capitol, about 1815, in an illustration from a late nineteenth-century history of the United States. *Library of Congress.*

because Dean was learning that slavery in Maryland was not ending just yet. Dean was not the first to make the ironic observation, "How much longer shall these outrages upon human nature be permitted under the very shadow of the Capitol?"

Dean was indignant that some Maryland slave owners who hired out bondsmen in D.C. intended not to comply with the pending bill. Dean's article told the tragic story of Edith Duval, who was long employed in D.C. although her owner lived in Maryland. When Duval reluctantly answered the door one day in early April 1862, "she saw her master, and the sad truth was revealed to the family, that she was to be forced away, by the loud shrieks and wailings of the girl. She was taken away amid the tears and protestations of the family."

The Duval case energized Dean to turn from writing articles to taking action. Dean wanted to volunteer his services, as he put it, "to defend the helpless slave, against the harpies who seek to carry him off." He understood he was opposing public opinion—he had written his wife soon after his arrival in D.C. that "I have been utterly confounded at the extent of the proslavery feeling here both in and outside of the government."

The *Baltimore Sun* of May 21, 1862, derided Dean as a provocative outsider:

> *The "new dodge" of making it a question whether under the fugitive slave act of 1850 slaves escaping from States into the District of Columbia can legally be remanded to their masters, is, it seems, to be tested by some parties who have made themselves residents of the District. A case will be made on the petition of some of the following named fugitives now in jail, and for whom Marshal Lamon has warrants under the fugitive act....The Hon. John Dean of Brooklyn will be counsel for the petitioners.*

Given Dean's shaky economic situation, though, he could not work for free. William Lloyd Garrison's abolitionist newspaper the *Liberator* of May 30, 1862, explained how Dean could manage by referring to his employment by "a Committee of wealthy and respectable citizens." Presumably, it was the National Freedman's Relief Association of D.C., formed to support African American refugees, that was paying Dean's fees. It had a committee with a budget allotting $200 for legal intervention to protect fleeing bondsmen. Dean's mentor, Underwood, was president of this association.

Dean was admitted to practice before the D.C. Circuit Court on May 22, 1862. Immediately, he plunged into a short but intense period of legal battles on behalf of those fleeing bondsmen considered "fugitives" from the law under the 1850 Fugitive Slave Act. The act's commissioners appointed by the D.C. courts in April 1862 acted on the warrants issued to slave owners to regain their human property.

When Dean defended the case of freedom seeker "Stephen," it was a chance to test Dean's legal strategies against applicability of the Fugitive Slave Act in the District. Dean questioned the Union loyalty of Stephen's alleged owner, Charles Hill, and the dubious validity of the identification of Stephen as Hill's missing property. Unfortunately, Dean was not successful, and the commissioners ruled to return Stephen to enslavement in Prince George's County. At this point, Dean could foresee the consequences of his interference with Stephen. The *National Republican* of May 22, 1862,

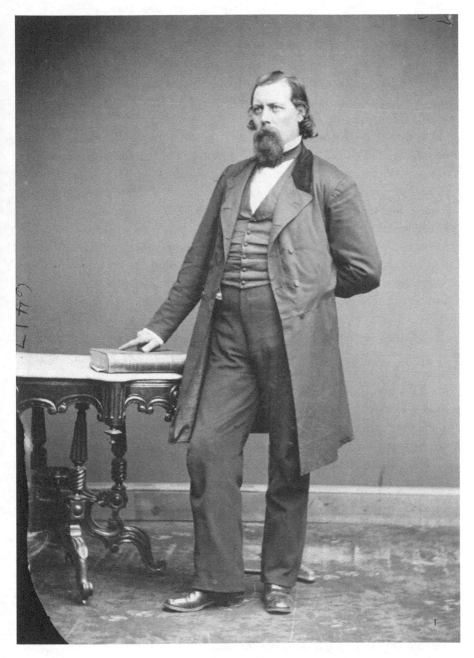

Ward H. Lamon, an old and devoted friend of Lincoln's, was appointed Marshal of D.C.
Library of Congress.

reported the conversation in which Dean appealed to Hill: "'I did not do it at the solicitation of the fugitive, and he is not to blame for any trouble which my acts have given you. I therefore ask that you will not whip this man; I beg of you not to do it.' Mr. Hill replied savagely, 'That is my business, and not yours!' and grasping his slave the 'master' bore off his 'property' in triumph."

That same day, Dean became involved in a well-publicized case defending Wilson Copeland from the claim of Ignatius H. Waters of Montgomery County at a hearing before Commissioner Walter Cox. Dean's visits to sick and wounded New York soldiers may have influenced his involvement; during the preceding month, Wilson Copeland and his companion, Alfred Johnson, had found refuge and jobs with the Seventy-Sixth New York Regiment. Its soldiers had blocked Marshal Ward Lamon's men from entering their camp in D.C., so Lamon's men had bided their time. After the regiment received transfer orders, Lamon's men stopped Copeland and Johnson in mid-march from the camp to the steamboat waiting on the Potomac River.

The *National Republican* of May 21, 1862, described what happened next. A large, excited crowd gathered, some soldiers were knocked down and other soldiers threatened to shoot into the crowd. To quiet the uproar, the regimental officers released Copeland and Johnson to Marshal Ward Lamon's men. The Seventy-Sixth's officers and soldiers protected other refugees sheltered by the regiment. Members of the regiment told the marshal that they "would see him in hell before they would deliver the negroes to him or any other person."

In order to intervene in the Copeland case, Dean presented a petition from Dr. Daniel Breed for a writ of habeas corpus. Breed, a fellow activist, was later imprisoned for seditious remarks in favor of insurrectionist John Brown. Dean argued that as army workers in uniform, Copeland and Johnson were government employees exempt from seizure under the Fugitive Slave Act. However, the judge postponed the decision, and Copeland and Johnson were sent to jail. The outcome was Copeland's return to slavery. During presentation of his argument, on May 29, Dean wrote his wife: "The Court is against me. It is like kicking against a stone wall."

It was not only the court that was hostile. On leaving the court, the *National Republican* reporter wrote on May 23, 1862, that he "saw any amount of ominous shaking of heads and brawny fists, and other outward manifestations of disapproval of the part Mr. D. took in the matter. Epithets and curses, 'not loud, but deep,' were heard on all sides. 'D—d abolitionist;' 'Every d—d abolitionist ought to have his throat cut;' 'I'd like to stuff all the niggers down their d—d throats.'" These were not the last threats Dean would receive. His efforts in court eventually put his life in danger.

Dean could count on the support of abolitionist and fellow New Yorker General James Wadsworth, appointed the district's military governor in April 1862 by President Lincoln. Wadsworth became an opponent of Marshal Lamon who, albeit proslavery, was a friend and former law partner of Lincoln. By allying himself with Wadsworth, Dean became enmeshed in the rivalry between Wadsworth and Lamon when Dean intervened on behalf of Alethia Lynch.

Barbara Allnutt of Montgomery County had claimed ownership of Lynch, with the result that the Fugitive Slave Commissioners had Lynch committed to jail. General Wadsworth intervened by ordering the provost guard to free Lynch after he had questioned Alnutt's loyalty to the Union. The

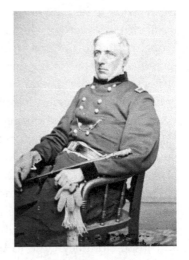

In 1862, Lincoln appointed General James S. Wadsworth as commander of the new Military District of Washington at a crucial moment during the debate over emancipation in the District. *Library of Congress.*

jailor, Benedict Milburn, and the deputy marshal, George Philips, refused to free Lynch without authorization from Lamon. Lynch was seized by force, and the tug-of-war between Wadsworth and Lamon began.

In order to free Lynch, the provost guard imprisoned the jailor, the deputy marshal and even Allnutt's attorney, Joseph Bradley, in the central guardhouse. The soldiers took over the D.C. jail. Learning what had transpired, Lamon tried with no result to see Lincoln. He then consulted the Attorney General. From the Attorney General, Lamon got leave to counter Wadsworth's move by arresting the military guards left behind at the jail. The standoff was not settled until the next morning with the release of those arrested and of Lynch.

Dean had the satisfaction of freeing Lynch. He took the precaution of keeping Lynch in hiding and giving her new papers. As Dean wrote in a letter to his wife on June 15, 1862, he was touched when "I gave her the Certificate of protection from the Genl. & she went forth with tears of joy on her ebony cheeks walking boldly home to her rightful employer."

It was tears that motivated Dean's intervention in the unsuccessful case of the brothers Bill and John Jackson, who were claimed by Dennis Duvall.

Dean wrote to his wife on June 11, 1862: "The tears that rolled down their black cheeks yesterday when I first found them in this Marshall's [sic] office brought tears to my eyes. And when I enquired about as to the cause of their weeping was gruffly answered by the claimant that it was none of my business. I told the claimant I would make it my business."

Dean came up against Joseph Bradley, who had been Allnutt's counsel and was temporarily jailed during the Lynch tug-of-war. Bradley, a prominent D.C. lawyer, was a slaveholder in favor of colonizing free African Americans outside the United States. Nonetheless, over his long years of practice in D.C., he worked for both African American and white antislavery activists. He represented Reuben Crandall in 1835 and Leonard Grimes in 1840, as well as slaveholders like Duvall and Allnutt.

The issue of owner Duvall's loyalty to the Union brought rivals Dean and Joseph Bradley close to blows. At one point, Dean was "ordered [by the court] to sit down or [he] would be put under arrest without any joint cause." Then, as Dean and Bradley confronted each other, the marshal had to intervene. Even so, Dean pronounced himself "cool as a cucumber" in a June 23 letter to his wife. According to the *National Republican* of May 28, 1862, Bradley then called the claimants "much more loyal than those who come to interfere with execution of the law." The court decided in Bradley's favor, and the Jacksons were returned to Duvall. On June 11, 1862, Dean's letter to his wife read: "After about 2 hours trial the two poor boys 'sons of Africa' were rendered up to slavery in Prince Geo. Co Maryland….And thus today we disposed of the exciting case and I bed [sic] the brothers goodbye."

Dean was trying to do the right thing by individual freedom seekers, but on June 5, 1862, he confessed in a letter to his wife that he was barely able to hold his temper in the face of insults. He gave an example of the case of Caroline Slater, a woman freed by the D.C. Emancipation Act who nonetheless was claimed as a bondswoman. Fugitive Slave Act commissioner Samuel Philips had threatened him with his cane and "said he would break my head etc etc" over their contradictory commands to the waiting driver of a carriage with Caroline Slater. Dean stopped himself but felt tempted to knock the proslavery Philips to the ground. Happily for Dean and Slater, Slater's claimants "backed out of the case."

There was a hiatus in Dean's legal activities as he found various means to pursue a livelihood. Dean was paid for a case in the U.S. Patent Office. Even though Dean told his wife on June 15, "I am kept very busy in this whirlpool of law; war; politics & philanthropy," he was pleased to be sworn into his Treasury job in the office of commissioner of customs on June 18, 1862.

32.   Thursday June 12th 1862

The Court met pursuant to adjournment

Present

Hon: {   James Dunlop   Chief Judge
         Jas. S. Morsell } Asst Judges
         Wm. M. Merrick }

Negroes John & William Jackson, fugitive slaves
owing labor & service to Dennis Duvall, of Prince
Georges County Maryland, were brought into
Court, under a Warrant of this Court, and after
examination was surrendered to his master under
the Fugitive Slave Law.

The Court adjourned until
Court in Course after a session of thirty two days—

The trial file contains information on the Jackson brothers, seized under the Fugitive
Slave Act and defended by John Dean. *Sandra Schmidt.*

At last, he was receiving a steady income he could share with his family. He was now too busy to take other Fugitive Slave Act cases but actively lobbied for creation of African American regiments. He also took up the cause of refugee Joseph Brooks in July by sending him to Dean's family in New York for work and an education.

In spring 1863, Lincoln created a D.C. Supreme Court with four judges handpicked by the president in the place of the previous circuit court's proslavery justices. Dean appeared in what was the first major case before the court and the last D.C. fugitive slave case.

Dean wrote home to his housekeeper on May 6, 1863, that he was going to try to present a petition for Dr. Breed for a writ of habeas corpus. Prior attempts to dismiss warrants of arrest of freedom seekers had failed. He hoped to finally be successful in his test of the law: "There are warrants out vs. about 200 fugitives. I am going to hunt up a case contest to question. The bar and the pro-slavery folks & slave catchers are again all in a rage at me etc."

Dean chose the case of Andrew Hall to test the law. Hall had escaped from Maryland the previous October and had been in D.C. ever since, according to the *Washington Evening Star* of May 12, 1863. George Washington Duvall of Prince George's County claimed him. Duvall was the son of Dennis Duvall, previously the claimant of the Jacksons.

Dean was retained as counsel to "Dr. Breed and others." On their behalf, he and co-counsel John Jolliffe presented a writ of habeas corpus for Andrew Hall on May 9. Jolliffe was an abolitionist lawyer from Ohio formerly involved in the Margaret Garner case. Joseph Bradley and past fugitive slave commissioner Walter Cox were attorneys for the claimant.

Dean's exalted motivation is evident in the summary of his argument he wrote for his daughter in a letter on May 14, 1863: "It is the great battle of freedom of humanity of Justice of Law that we are here this day fighting. We have elsewhere in this contest, bullets and bayonettes [sic] on our side, but [in] its absence, its great principle is here presented for victory or for defeat. What vast results hang upon the decisions of the single case!"

Dean's emotions again got Dean and Bradley into a fracas. When stymied because Hall was to be discharged and leave the courtroom, Duvall, backed by some friends, seized Hall by the collar. Dean and his co-counsel, John Joliffe, resisted. When the fugitive was again taken into the judge's room, Dean asked for Duvall to be punished for stopping the "operations of the court."

Outside, the owner and friends muttered about whose side was more law-abiding and contributed more money to the Union. A rumor passed through the crowd that Dean would be arrested for assault and battery. In the meantime, the military authorities intervened by taking charge of Hall at the police station house where he had been taken. They protected him with a military guard and sent him to a contraband camp. He promptly enlisted and later died a soldier's death. According to records of D.C.'s First Regiment U.S. Colored Troops, Private Andrew Hall, a farmer from Prince George's County, died at Point of Rocks in Maryland in 1864.

Dean was frightened by the continuing public response to the Hall case. He confided to his wife on May 25, 1863:

> *The rage of the Marylanders and proslavery men is at the highest pitch vs. me. I am insulted in the streets by them and they seek every occasion to bring on a collision, but I do not notice them and am not out nights unless some one is with me. The boy Andrew Hall is enlisted. I am however sustained by our radical friends. And if any misfortune in the contest befalls me, you and the dear ones* [his family] *I think will be provided for....I suppose it likely I shall be sued by Duvall.*

Dean and co-defending lawyer John Jolliffe were indeed indicted for assault and battery in June 1863; each had to present $1,000 bail. Underwood, now a judge, covered bail for Jolliffe. Dean, however, decided to take advantage of his ties to the African American community. They were derived from his participation in the drive for recruitment of the U.S. Colored Troops and exploration of a for-profit scheme for colonization of African Americans outside the United States. On June 7, 1863, Dean wrote to his wife, "A negro [Bowen] has agreed to be my bail & I prefer him to a white man under the circumstances of the case."

Apparently, Jolliffe, brought into the case after Dean, had plans to use the trial as a "show trial" involving prominent national antislavery leaders like Gerrit Smith, Wendell Phillips and Charles Sumner. Dean, on the other hand, resolved to retaliate against the indictment by requesting a revocation both of the warrant against Hall and of the re-appointment of Walter Cox, formerly a counsel for Allnutt and a fugitive slave commissioner. Dean was working on the case for revocation in late May.

Scheduled for the October 1863 term of the criminal court, the trial did not occur. In early October, John Dean died of pneumonia at his rented rooms on Sixth Street between E and F Streets. In its obituary, the *Evening Star* of October 16, 1863, remembered Dean by saying that when he arrived in the district at the time of D.C. emancipation, "he entered at

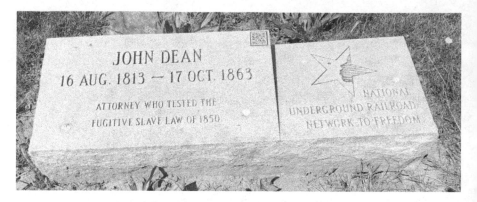

John Dean's grave lies in the Congressional Cemetery, Washington, D.C. *Sandra Schmidt.*

once energetically into the business of defending it, and securing negroes their rights under it." At the funeral, his pallbearers were Underwood, coworkers at the Treasury Department and fellow members of the National Freedman's Relief Association of D.C., Daniel Goodloe and George E. Day. The African American community had been preparing since January to give Dean an inscribed gold-headed cane in gratitude and instead had to present it to his widow.

Without Dean, in the first year of the new Supreme Court, fifteen fugitives went back into slavery, although the Andrew Hall case was the last 1850 Fugitive Slave Act case tried in D.C. before the act was repealed. Thanks to the intervention of the military and of crowds supporting "fugitives," the act was not further enforced. The Fugitive Slave Act continued to be applicable in D.C. and Maryland until June 1864, although slavery in Maryland lasted a few months more.

10

SHORT PROFILES

There are only two chapters above and two sketches in this section. Missing are more members of the African American community partly because of African American participants' care with anonymity and the need to further explore oral traditions.

YARDLEY TAYLOR:
WITH GOOSE CREEK MEETING BEHIND HIM

There's a curious document from July 1857 at the Thomas Balch Library in Leesburg, Virginia. It is a broadside by James Trayhern lambasting someone named Yardley Taylor located in Loudoun County near what is now called Lincoln. Portrayed as a "square built, heavy set, hugely footed, not very courtly figure of an old man," Taylor would have been unmistakable if encountered delivering Goose Creek's mail. Despite Taylor's seemingly innocent "demure visage and meditative air," Trayhern accused him of association with the "affairs of the Underground Railroad Company," of being "Chief of the abolition clan in Loudoun" and of having admitted to helping an escaping bondsman.

When, in 2016, Lee Lawrence found Taylor's court records in the archives of the Loudoun County Courthouse, they explained Trayhern's accusations. Taylor figured in a trial in 1830 (when he would have been about thirty-three years old) and was convicted for enticing a freedom seeker named Harry to escape in 1828. Harry was on the run from Samuel Cox of Loudoun County, who had hired his services from Mrs. Allison of Stafford County, Virginia. Following word that Allison was considering selling him, Harry took the risk and decided to flee north.

Harry had bad luck. Slave catchers not only caught Harry but also seized an incriminating letter he was carrying signed by Yardley Taylor. The sheriff issued a warrant for Taylor's arrest on the basis of Taylor's recommendation of Harry to the care of Jonathan Jessup in York, Pennsylvania. A free African American man, Alex McPherson, had risked loaning his freedom certificate to

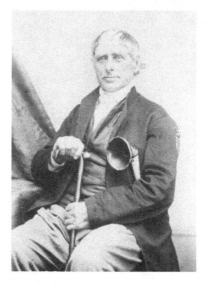

Yardley Taylor was tried for helping Harry to escape. *Courtesy of the Loudoun Museum.*

the conspirators in order to give Harry the credentials needed to travel freely. Captured along with the letter was a crude map with mileage to or from various points on Harry's route. After Taylor pleaded not guilty, his case continued for two years until he finally changed his plea and paid a twenty-dollar fine.

Yardley Taylor is buried at Goose Creek Burying Ground by the Goose Creek Quaker Meetinghouse in Virginia. As befits a Quaker, the gravestone is simple, providing no epitaph. In the broadside, Trayhern did not mention either that Taylor was a Quaker or the differences between the Quakers and their neighbors.

On the one hand, Taylor was an active member of the Lincoln business community, as he owned a local nursery called Springdale, specializing in fruit trees. He was a respected surveyor and mapmaker, producing a very good map of the county in 1853.

On the other, as an active member of Goose Creek Friends Meeting, he belonged to a group that rejected slavery and saw it as evil enough to justify breaking the law. Like other Quakers, Taylor wore "plain dress," that is, simple black garments including a wide-brimmed hat, and would address other people as "thee" and "thou." He would be held to tell the truth, to respect every man—African American or white, enslaved or free. Because of the organization of Quaker meetings, he would have had frequent contact with fellow Quakers in nearby communities, and because of the necessity of marrying within the faith, he would have had relatives scattered throughout regional meetings. In the broadside, there was a clash of worldviews as well as morality between Trayhern and Taylor.

WILLIAM BOYD:
DOCTOR OF UNDERGROUND-RAILROAD-OLOGY

It did not take some immigrants long in this country before they realized slavery was an abomination. In one case, it only took a couple of years after his arrival for the immigrant to undertake risks as an operative of the Underground Railroad. An Irishman described by the *Evening Star* of November 21, 1858, as "a small thin, sharp nosed dispeptic [*sic*] looking, sandy whiskered genius, say about 118 lbs. Weight" was caught on November 2, 1858. He was accompanied by two anonymous freedom seekers at New Windsor, Carroll County, Maryland, about fifteen miles from Pennsylvania. Although a tailor, Boyd was called "Dr." He justified his journeys to facilitate escape as visits to rural areas to buy herbal medicines and produce to peddle from his horse-drawn wagon. He was able to hide freedom seekers in the wagon in a space hidden by black curtains that created the illusion of being the back of the wagon.

Susan E. Holmes and William R. Russell from Washington were the claimants of the two freedom seekers, a woman and a man, with whom Boyd was caught. After a brief jailing in Westminster, Maryland, Dr. Boyd was taken to Washington and indicted by a grand jury on two counts of stealing and two counts of transporting bondsmen to a free state. According to one claimant (called both Mrs. Howell and Susan E. Holmes), she discovered the flight of her missing woman one hour after the woman had waited on the dinner table on October 16. The next the owner knew was when she was informed that someone fitting the description of her property was jailed in Westminster for having broken the law as a "runaway slave." The woman that Mrs. Howell (or Holmes) identified had lived with her about three years and was married to the man enslaved by Major Russell. The woman's enslaved husband was allowed to hire himself out and to live in a room on G Street, but Mrs. Holmes had found no sign of her woman there.

Dr. Boyd was further incriminated. First, there was a letter from Westminster stating, "The white man is fully identified as the man who was with Col. Lee's black" in spring 1858. Second, someone else provided testimony that when he had seen Boyd driving off the road twice, he supposed Dr. Boyd was trying to avoid identification. Boyd was convicted on two counts of "stealing slaves." When he received a fourteen-year sentence for larceny, the news spread even to newspapers in Georgia. Dr. Boyd only had to serve a little over a year and a half. In October 1861, he was pardoned by President Lincoln on the basis of good behavior in prison and prior good character. His imprisonment probably ended Boyd's career with the Underground Railroad; within a few months, Congress emancipated bondsmen living in D.C.

CONCLUSION

These stories of Underground Railroad heroes in the Washington area are meant to represent the many accounts that cannot yet be pieced together. For every story rescued from oblivion, there are hundreds that may be lost. Just as it takes cooperation to resist slavery through flight, it takes cooperation as well as patience to put together pieces of Underground Railroad history. The stories for which there is evidence are not just good yarns. These documented stories can be a legacy of pride for people of all races. That means that it is important to separate fact from fiction.

Romance and secrecy may be the first draw to the subject of the Underground Railroad. Another draw is the appeal of the heroes who, like all heroes, inspire and act as examples. The heroes can serve as models for cooperation of people of all backgrounds toward the common goals of respect, freedom and equal rights.

The heroes are remarkable for the lengths to which they were willing to go without giving up. They dreamed big dreams. They were willing to stretch the categories of what was allowed for their color, gender and position. They showed endurance, courage and resourcefulness. They were daring and took risky decisions in an attempt to control their fates. They believed that they could make a difference and be successful in their goals. They were willing to see beyond the norms accepted at the time and to obey a moral law taking precedence over the American Constitution and courts. They recognized humanity in those considered less than human and realized that it was a trick of fate as to who ended up white and free and who African American and unfree.

CONCLUSION

The book's chapters should help to reshape the myths of the Underground Railroad and slavery. Emphasis on the exploits of white accomplices can make us forget the great risk of an unhappy ending that faced the Africans and African Americans who dared to flee slavery. These accounts of flight to freedom do not depend on the standard elements of Underground Railroad myth. There are no secret hiding places, hidden tunnels, quilts or secret codes. There are no regular "stations," although there are places from which people disappeared as if on an underground train. Instead, there are cornfields, cemeteries and designated spots to meet or to hide briefly. Not all freedom seekers traveled on foot through the forest. These narratives describe how those escaping also traveled on ships, in wagons with hiding places, in carriages on toll roads and on railroad trains. There was plenty of resourcefulness and ingenuity—disguises, stowing away on ships, forgeries and passing for free. Instead of quilts with secret codes, there were letters and word of mouth through extended social networks. As in legend, activists planned and arranged, escorted and provided or indicated hiding places. They also financed operations, put up bail and defended freedom seekers in court. Activists were moved by the stories of the freedom seekers and used them in newspaper articles, lectures and slave narratives. They generated support by demonstrating characteristics that enslaved African Americans had in common with those whose sympathy activists sought.

The events of resistance to slavery strike twenty-first-century readers as earth-shattering moments to admire and emulate. It is necessary to remember that the subjects of these chapters were human and complex. Without trust in God and/or their fellow man, they would have found it impossible to proceed. Those fleeing or enabling the freedom seekers hoped, but did not know for sure, that their decisions and journeys would change American society forever. It may not have seemed glorious at the time—rather, uncertain and frightening. The unknown loomed, and there was physical danger. It may have been only after the fact that these heroes realized that they had arrived at a climactic moment of their lives when resisting slavery.

The Underground Railroad has importance today because it is part of the unfinished American racial struggle for civil rights. In a broader sense, as people continue to seek freedom all over the world, the history of the Underground Railroad provides an important example of people of different races, ethnic backgrounds and religious faiths working together for a common cause as yet unattained. The heroes in the Washington area overcame their despair at inhumane conditions long enough to resist.

Appendix

NATIONAL UNDERGROUND RAILROAD NETWORK TO FREEDOM PROGRAM, NATIONAL CAPITAL REGION, NATIONAL PARK SERVICE

DISTRICT OF COLUMBIA (WASHINGTON, D.C.)

MEMBER NAME AND ADDRESS	MEMBER TYPE
African American Civil War Memorial 1000 U Street NW 20009	Site
Asbury United Methodist Church 11th and K Streets NW 20001	Site
Blanche K. Bruce Burial Site (Woodlawn Cemetery) 4611 Benning Road SE 20017	Site
Blanche K. Bruce House (private)	Site
Camp Greene and Contraband Camp Theodore Roosevelt Island, Potomac River (access from Virginia)	Site
Frederick Douglass National Historic Site 1411 W Street SE 20020	Site
John Little Farm Site, Kalorama Park Kalorama Road and 19th Street NW 20009	Site
Leonard Grimes Property Site (plaque) 22nd and H Street NW 20052	Site
Mary Ann Shadd Cary House (private)	Site

Member Name and Address	Member Type
Moorland-Spingarn Research Center, Howard University, Founders Library 500 Howard Place NW 20059	Facility
Mt. Pleasant Plains Cemetery at Kalorama Park 20009 (between Calvert Street and Adams Mill Road NW, Rock Creek and the National Zoo)	Site
Old City Hall, 451 Indiana Avenue NW 20001	Site
William Boyd, John Dean, David A. Hall, and Hannibal Hamlin Burial Sites at Congressional Cemetery 1801 E Street SE 20003	Site
Washingtoniana Division, D.C. Public Library 901 G Street NW 20001	Facility
From Slavery to Freedom, African American Civil War Museum and Foundation 1925 Vermont Avenue NW 20001	Program
Slavery and the Underground Railroad with a Focus on the Nation's Capital, White House Visitor Center, 1450 Pennsylvania Avenue NW 20230	Program

MARYLAND

Member Name and Address	Member Type
Belair Mansion 12207 Tulip Grove Drive, Bowie 20715	Site
Berry Farm at Oxon Cove Farm 6411 Oxon Hill Road, Oxon Hill 20745	Site
Best Farm/L'Hermitage, Monocacy National Battlefield 4801 Urbana Pike, Frederick 21704	Site
Catoctin Iron Furnace and Manor House Ruins Cunningham Falls State Park 14039 Catoctin Hollow Road, Thurmont 21788	Site
Chesapeake and Ohio Canal, Chesapeake & Ohio Canal NHP, 1850 Dual Highway, Suite 100, Hagerstown 21740 Runs from Georgetown (D.C.) to Cumberland (MD).	Site

MEMBER NAME AND ADDRESS	MEMBER TYPE
Darnall's Chance 14800 Governor Oden Bowie Drive, Upper Marlboro 20772	Site
Elizabeth Keckly Burial Site, National Harmony Memorial Park 7101 Sheriff Road, Largo 20792	Site
Ferry Hill Plantation, Chesapeake & Ohio Canal National Historic Park 16500 Shepherdstown Pike, Sharpsburg 21782	Site
Freedom Site of Emily Plummer (Riversdale) Riversdale House Museum 4811 Riverdale Road, Riverdale Park 20737	Site
Marietta House 5626 Bell Station Road, Glenn Dale 20769	Site
Mount Calvert Historical and Archaeological Park 16302 Mount Calvert Road, Upper Marlboro 20772	Site
Mouth of Swan Creek Escape Site 13551 Fort Washington Road, Fort Washington 20744 (In the water across from Fort Washington by Diggs Point)	Site
Northampton Slave Quarters and Archaeological Park Lake Overlook Drive, Bowie 20721	Site
Port Tobacco Courthouse 8430 Commerce Street, Port Tobacco 20677	Site
Josiah Henson Park (Montgomery Parks) 11420 Old Georgetown Road, Rockville 20852	Site
Rockland (private)	Site
Sotterley 44300 Sotterley Lane, Hollywood 20636	Site
Thornton Poole House (private)	Site
William Chaplin Arrest Site, Jesup Blair Local Park (Montgomery Parks) Georgia Avenue and D.C. Line, Silver Spring 20910	Site

MEMBER NAME AND ADDRESS	MEMBER TYPE
Jane C. Sween Library, Montgomery Co. Historical Society 111 West Montgomery Avenue, Rockville 20850	Facility
Maryland State Archives 350 Rowe Boulevard, Annapolis 21401	Facility
In Their Steps, Peerless Rockville Historic Preservation, Ltd. 29 Courthouse Square, Rockville 20850	Program
Underground Railroad Experience Trail Hike Woodlawn Manor Cultural Park (Montgomery Parks) 16501 Norwood Road, Sandy Spring 20860	Program

Virginia

MEMBER NAME AND ADDRESS	MEMBER TYPE
Alexandria Freedmen's Cemetery 1001 South Washington Street, Alexandria 22313	Site
Arlington House, Robert E. Lee Memorial 32 Sherman Drive, Fort Myer 22211 (by Arlington National Cemetery)	Site
Birch Slave Pen (Freedom House Museum) 1315 Duke Street, Alexandria 22314	Site
Brentsville Courthouse and Jail 12229 Bristow Road, Bristow 20136	Site
Bruin's Slave Jail (private)	Site
Buckland Farm (private)	Site
Conn's Ferry, Riverbend Park 8700 Potomac Hills Street, Great Falls 22066	Site
Evergreen (private)	Site
Freedmen's Aid Workers Site (private)	Site
Gadsby's Tavern Museum 134 North Royal Street, Alexandria 22314	Site
Leesylvania, Leesylvania State Park 2001 Daniel K. Ludwig Drive, Woodridge 22191	Site

MEMBER NAME AND ADDRESS	MEMBER TYPE
Loudoun County Courthouse 18 East Market Street, Leesburg 20176	Site
Melrose Farm (private)	Site
Oatlands Plantation 20850 Oatlands Plantation Lane, Leesburg 20175 (Route 15, six miles south of Leesburg)	Site
Old Jail (Fauquier History Museum) 10 Ashby Street, Warrenton 22186	Site
Rippon Lodge 15520 Blackburn Road, Woodbridge 22191	Site
Sully Historic Site 3601 Sully Road, Chantilly 20151	Site
Afro-American Historical Association of Fauquier County 4243 Loudoun Avenue, The Plains 20198	Facility
Alexandria Archaeology Museum (Torpedo Factory Art Center) 105 North Union Street #327, Alexandria 22314	Facility
Alexandria Library, Local History/Special Collections 717 Queen Street, Alexandria 22314	Facility
Fairfax Circuit Court—Historical Records Center 4110 Chain Bridge Road, Suite 315, Fairfax 22030	Facility
Library of Virginia 800 East Broad Street, Richmond 23219	Facility
Thomas Balch Library 208 West Market Street, Leesburg 20176	Facility
Virginia Historical Society 428 North Boulevard, Richmond 23220	Facility

Member types:
Site = place
Facility = museum, library or archive
Program = educational program
For more information, visit http://www.nps.gov/ugrr.

SELECTED SOURCES

Background

Bancroft, Frederic Bancroft. *Slave Trading in the Old South*. Columbia: University of South Carolina Press, 1996.

Blassingame, John W., ed. *Slave Testimony: Two Centuries of Letters, Speeches, Interviews, and Autobiographies*. Baton Rouge: Louisiana State University Press, 1977.

Field, Barbara Jeanne. *Slavery and Freedom on the Middle Ground: Maryland During the Nineteenth Century*. New Haven, CT: Yale University Press, 1985.

Finkelman, Paul, and Donald R. Kennon, eds. *In the Shadow of Freedom: The Politics of Slavery in the National Capital*. Published for the United States Capitol Historical Society. Athens: Ohio University Press, 2011.

Fleischner, Jennifer. *Mrs. Lincoln and Mrs. Keckly: The Remarkable Story of the Friendship Between a First Lady and a Former Slave*. New York: Broadway Books, 2003.

Graham, Lawrence Otis. *The Senator and the Socialite*. New York: Harper Perennial, 2006.

Green, Constance McLaughlin. *Secret City: A History of Race Relations in the Nation's Capital*. Princeton, NJ: Princeton University Press, 1967.

———. *Washington: A History of the Capital, 1800–1950*. Princeton, NJ: Princeton University Press, 1962.

Harrold, Stanley. *Subversives: Antislavery Community in Washington, DC, 1828–1865*. Baton Rouge: Louisiana State University Press, 2003.

Hudson, J. Blaine. *Encyclopedia of the Underground Railroad*. Jefferson, NC: McFarland & Co., 2006.

Kolchin, Peter. *American Slavery, 1619–1877*. New York: Hill and Wang, 1993.

National Underground Railroad Network to Freedom, National Park Service, Applications, 2000–2015.

Northup, Solomon. *Twelve Years a Slave: Narrative of Solomon Northup, a Citizen of New-York, Kidnapped in Washington City in 1841, and Rescued in 1853*. Auburn: Derby & Miller, 1853. http://www.docsouth.unc.edu/fpn/northup/northup.html.

Oakes, James. *The Scorpion's Sting: Antislavery and the Coming of the Civil War*. New York: W.W. Norton & Co., 2014.

Pacheco, Josephine F. *The Pearl: A Failed Slave Escape on the Potomac*. Chapel Hill: University of North Carolina Press, 2005.

Ricks, Mary Kay. *Escape on the* Pearl*: The Heroic Bid for Freedom on the Underground Railroad*. New York: William Morrow, 2007.

Russell, Hilary. *Final Research Report: The Operation of the Underground Railroad in Washington, D.C., c. 1800–1860*. Washington, D.C.: A product of a cooperative agreement between the Historical Society of Washington and the National Park Service, July 2001.

Sinha, Manisha. *The Slave's Cause: A History of Abolition*. New Haven, CT: Yale University Press, 2016.

Smallwood, Thomas. *A Narrative of Thomas Smallwood*. City Buildings: James Stephens, 1851. http://www.doc.unc.edu/neh/smallwood/smallwood.htm.

Stowe, Harriet Beecher. *A Key to Uncle Tom's Cabin*. Bedford, MA: Applewood Books, n.d., reprint of 1852, 1853.

Mary and Arthur Cooper

Encyclopedia of Virginia. "Commonwealth of Massachusetts versus Camillus Griffith (1823)." Encyclopediavirginia.org. Virginia Humanities in partnership with Library of Virginia.

Fairfax County, Virginia. Court Order Book, 1822, 183.

———. Superior Court Order Book 1819, May 27, 1823.

Gara, Larry. *The Liberty Line: The Legend of the Underground Railroad*. Lexington: University of Kentucky, 1961.

Gardner, Grace Brown. "Fifty Famous Nantucketers." *Inquirer and Mirror*, June 3, 1950.

Grover, Kathryn. *The Fugitive's Gibraltar: Escaping Slaves and Abolitionism in New Bedford, Massachusetts*. Amherst: University of Massachusetts Press, 2001.

————. *Fugitive Slave Traffic and the Maritime World of New Bedford*. New Bedford, MA: New Bedford Whaling Museum and Boston Support Office, National Park Service, 1998. http://www.npshistory.com/publications/nebe/grover.pdf.

Hartford Courant. "Fugitive Slaves in Nantucket." March 2, 1901 (from *New Bedford Standard*).

Inquirer and Mirror (Nantucket). "An Anti-slavery Pioneer." December 3, 1887.

————. "The Arthur Cooper Case." May 4, 1878.

————. "Kidnapping at Nantucket." October 24, 1822.

————. "Kidnapping in Nantucket." October 29, 1822.

————. Letter to editor. June 15, 1878.

————. "Looking Backward." June 6, 1996.

————. "Mrs. Lucy Cooper—The Slave Who Died in Her 110th Year." January 25, 1936.

————. "Nantucket Argonauts Sailed for California 100 years Ago." January 8, 1949.

————. "Nantucket's Proud History of Tolerance." February 25, 2010.

————. "Obituary: Gardner." February 23, 1886.

————. "Old and New Nantucket." August 30, 1879.

————. "The Quakers and Slavery." March 16, 1878.

————. "Randolph Cooper." February 1, 1890.

————. "When Arthur Cooper Fled to Nantucket for Protection." December 15, 1917.

Islander. "Advertisement as Barber by Arthur Cooper, Jr." November 5, 1842.

Island Review (Nantucket). "Quakers and Slavery." March 27, 1878.

————. "Quakers and Slavery." March 30, 1878.

Johnson, Robert. "Black-White Relations on Nantucket." *Historic Nantucket* 51, no. 2 (2002): 5–9.

Karttunen, Frances. E-mail to author, October 24, 2017.

————. "Letterbag: An Amazing Discovery." *Inquirer and Mirror*. February 15, 2007.

————. *Other Islanders: People Who Pulled the Oars*. Nantucket, MA: Nantucket Historical Association, 2005.

————. Personal communication, May 13, 2018.

————. "Writing History of Nantucket's Immigrants." *Inquirer and Mirror*. July 12, 1973.

Liberator. "A Voice from Nantucket." August 20, 1831.

Macy, Thomas Mackrell [sic]. "Account of slave in the State House, Massachusetts which occurred in Nantucket in 1822." Transcription at Nantucket Historical Association, Nantucket, Massachusetts. MS 222-4-1.

Monaghan, James. "Anti-Slavery in Nantucket." In *Proceedings of the Nantucket Historical Association*, 44th Annual Meeting, Nantucket, July 1938.

National Park Service. *Behind the Mansions: The Political, Economic, and Social Life of a New Bedford Neighborhood, County-Sixth Neighborhood Study.* May 2006. https://www.nps.gov/subjects/ugrr/discover_history/upload/nebebehindmansions.pdf.

Netherton, Nan, Donald Sweig, Janice Artemal, Patricia Hicken and Patrick Read. *Fairfax County, Virginia, a History.* Fairfax, VA: Fairfax County Board of Supervisors, 1992.

Pariseau, Justin Andrew. E-mail message to author, October 19, 2017.

———. "Sea of Change: Race, Abolitionism, and Reform in the New England Whale Fishery." PhD diss., College of William and Mary, 2015.

———. "Seizing Agency: Black Nantucket and the Abolitionist Press, 1832–48." *Historic Nantucket* 52, no. 4 (2003): 11–16.

Republican Standard (New Bedford). "Quakers and Slavery: A Fugitive Slave Case in New Bedford Fifty Years Ago." May 14, 1878.

Stackpole, Edouard A. "'Angola Street' and Arthur Cooper—A Misplaced Street and a Rescued Slave." In *Proceedings of the Nantucket Historical Association*, 47th Annual Meeting, July 29, 1941.

Sweig, Donald M. *Slavery in Fairfax County, VA 1750–1860.* Fairfax County, VA: History and Archaeology Section Office of Comprehensive Planning, June 1983.

U.S. Census, 1810–1860. Heads of Families. Washington, D.C.

White, Barbara. "Arthur Cooper." In Henry Louis Gates and Evelyn Brooks Higginbotham, *African American National Biography*, 2nd ed., vol. 3. Oxford: Oxford University Press, 2013.

———. Personal communication, May 14, 2018.

Worrall, Arthur J. *Quaker Nantucket: The Religion Behind the Whale Empire.* Nantucket, MA: Mill Hill Press, 1997.

Anna Maria Gant

Biographical and Historical Memoirs of Muskingum County, Ohio. Chicago: Goodspeed Publishing Company, 1892.

Christian Recorder. "A Plain Statement." December 8, 1866.

Christian Register. "Trial for Wife Stealing." January 30, 1847.

Cleveland Gazette. "Nelson T. Gant, Sr., Dead." July 29, 1905.

Dollings, Raymond. "Rivals Romance." *Zanesville Courier*, November 17, 1894.

Loudoun County, Virginia. Misc. Paper—Criminal Case: Gant, Talbot Nelson—Free Blacks.

National Era. "An Interesting and Important Decision." January 7, 1847.

Nelson T. Gant to Dr. Francis Julius LeMoyne, June 7, 1847, Washington County, Pennsylvania, Historical Society, Washington, Pennsylvania.

New York Evangelist. "Can a Slave Be Lawfully Married?" February 11, 1847.

Payne, Daniel. "Biographical Sketch of Mrs. Anna Maria Gant." *Christian Recorder*, April 11, 1878.

Rawson, Eliza R. "Worthy Friends of the Nineteenth Century: Samuel M. Janney." *Friends Intelligencer*, May 20, 1899.

Robinson, Victoria J., "Registered in the Chancery of Heaven: The Marriage of Nelson Talbot and Anna Maria Hughes." *Getting to the "Roots" of the Problem: A Genealogical Journey in Harvesting the Past* (blog). www.vicjorob. blogspot.com.

———. "Nixon's Slaves." *Getting to the "Roots" of the Problem: A Genealogical Journey in Harvesting the Past* (blog). http://www.vicjorob.blogspot.com.

———. Personal conversations, July 2017.

Schneider, Morris F. "The Story of Nelson T. Gant." *Zanesville Sunday-Times-Signal*, April 4, 1946.

Ann Maria Weems

Chester Times. "Dr. Ellwood Harvey." March 4, 1880.

Cleveland, Emmeline. "Reminiscences." *Forney's Progress* 1, no. 8 (1879): 152–153.

Cohen, Anthony B. *The Underground Railroad in Montgomery County, Maryland: A History and Driving Guide*. Rockville, MD: Montgomery County Historical Society, 1994.

Marshall, Clara. *The Women's Medical College of Pennsylvania: An Historical Outline*. Philadelphia: P. Blakiston Son, 1897.

Prince, Bryan. *A Shadow on the Household: One Enslaved Family's Incredible Struggle for Freedom*. Toronto: McClelland & Stewart, 2009.

Ray, F.T. *Sketch of the Life of Rev. Charles B. Ray*. New York: Press of J.J. Little & Co., 1887.

Ripley, C. Peter, et al. *The Black Abolitionist Papers.* Chapel Hill: University of North Carolina, 1991. Black Abolitionist Papers, 1830–1865, on microfilm, reel 7: *Anti-Slavery Reporter,* December 1, 1852; *Christian News,* November 11, 1853; *Non-Conformist,* November 17, 1852.

Still, William. "Boy, Thanksgiving Day, November 22, 1855," Journal C of Station No. 2: 229-231, Pennsylvania Abolition Society Papers, Historical Society of Pennsylvania. http://www.hsp.org

———. *The Underground Railroad.* 1871. Ebony Classics Chicago: Johnson Publishing Company, 1970 [reprint].

Swift, David E. *Prophets of Justice: Activists Before the Civil War.* Baton Rouge: Louisiana State University Press, 1989.

Tappan, Lewis. Letter to Jacob Bigelow. December 3, 1855. Letterbook, Lewis Tappan Papers, Library of Congress, Washington, D.C.

———. Letter to Jacob Bigelow. December 6, 1855. Letterbook, Lewis Tappan Papers, Library of Congress, Washington, D.C.

———. December 6, 1855. Letterbook, Lewis Tappan Papers, Library of Congress, Washington, D.C.

———. Letter to Ellwood Harvey. December 3, 1855. Letterbook, Lewis Tappan Papers, Library of Congress, Washington, D.C.

———. Letter to Ellwood Harvey. December 4, 1855. Letterbook, Lewis Tappan Papers, Library of Congress, Washington, D.C.

Tappan, Sarah. Letter to Henry Richardson. December 8, 1855. Letterbook, Lewis Tappan Papers, Library of Congress, Washington, D.C.

Work, M.N. "The Life of Charles B. Ray." *Journal of Negro History* 4, no. 4 (1919): 361–371.

Emily Plummer

"Adam Frances Plummer Diary." Anacostia Community Museum, Smithsonian Institution, Washington, D.C. http://www.anacostia.si.edu/exhibits/Plummer/Plummer_Home.htm.

Baltimore Slave Jail Records. Docket No. 824. "Committed as Runaway: Emma Blumbe." Legacy of Slavery in Maryland, Maryland State Archives, Annapolis, Maryland. http://www.slavery2.msa.maryland.gov.

Donaldson, Thomas, to Charles Benedict Calvert, October 5 and 13, 1863, anonymous collection (on loan), Riversdale House Museum, Prince George's County, Maryland.

Hendricks, Charlie. "Anacostia Museum Posts Diary of Riversdale's Adam Francis Plummer." *News and Notes, Prince George's County Historical Society* 36, no. 1 (2008): 1, 3.

"Letters of Negroes, Largely Personal and Private [Part I]. Authors include Adam Plummer, Sarah Miranda Plummer, Emily Plumer [sic]." *The Journal of Negro History* 11, no. 1 (1926): 62–87.

Plummer, Nellie Arnold. *Out of the Depths, or, the Triumph of the Cross*. Hyattsville, MD: 1927.

Ryan, Leigh. "The Extraordinary Life of Emily Saunders Plummer, Riversdale." *Riversdale Historical Society Newsletter* (Spring 2016).

Woodson, Carter G., ed. *Mind of the Negro as Reflected in Letters Written During the Crisis 1800–1860*. Washington, DC: Association for the Study of Negro Life and History, 1926. New York: Negro Universities Press, 1969 [reprint].

Billy

"Col. John Tayloe to Col. Landon Carter," March 31, 1771. Geography of Slavery. http://www2.vcdh.virginia.edu.

"Mann Page on Behalf of Billy and enclosure." May 13, 1781. *In Papers of Thomas Jefferson*, February 25, 1781–May 20, 1781, Julian P. Boyd, ed. Princeton, NJ: Princeton University Press, 1952, 5: 640–643.

Maryland Gazette (Green). "Runaway Slave Ad." April 4, 1765. Geography of Slavery. http://www2.vcdh.virginia.edu.

"A Petition of Mann Page on Behalf of Billy." June 7, 1781. Legislative Petitions, Prince William County, Record Group 78, Library of Virginia, Richmond, Virginia.

Proceedings of a Court of Oyer and Terminer. May 8, 1781. Prince William County, Virginia.

Pybus, Cassandra. *Epic Journeys of Freedom*. Boston: Beacon Press, 2006.

Schwarz, Phillip J. "Billy." Contributed by the Dictionary of Virginia Biography to Encyclopedia of Virginia. http://www.encyclopediavirginia. org.

Taylor, Alan. *Internal Enemy: Slavery and War in Virginia, 1772–1832*. New York: W.W. Norton, 2013.

Hortense Prout

Belcher, Mary. "Site of John Little's Manor House." Application, National Underground Network to Freedom. July 9, 2008.

Washington Evening Star. "A Fugitive." June 17, 1861.

Bill Wheeler and Mark Caesar

Hardy, Cathy. "Port Tobacco Courthouse." Application, National Underground Railroad Network to Freedom. January 15, 2005.

Maryland State Archives. (Biographical Series) Mark Caesar: Accomplice to Slave Flight. Charles County, Maryland, 1845. MSA SC 549003364. http://www.msa.maryland.gov.

———. William "Bill" Wheeler: Accomplice to Slave Flight. Charles County, MD, 1845. MSA SC 5496-15156. http://www.msa.maryland.gov.

Maria Bear Toliver

Department of Interior. Official Register of Officers and Employes [sic] in the Civil, Military and Naval Service. Vol. I. Washington, DC: Government Printing Office, 1879.

Schulz, Jane E. "Seldom Thanked, Never Praised, and Scarcely Recognized: Gender and Racism in Civil War Hospitals." *Civil War History* 48 (2002), no. 3: 220–236.

U.S. Civil War Pension Files. Mary Toliver. National Archives, Washington, DC. Application no. 1161879.

Mrs. Sprigg's Boardinghouse

Barnes, Gilbert H., and Dwight L. Dumond, eds. *Letters of Theodore Dwight Weld, Angelina Grimke Weld and Sarah Grimke, 1822–1844.* 2 vols. New York: D. Appleton-Century, 1934.

Brooks, Corey. "Stoking the 'Abolition Fire in the Capitol': Liberty Party Lobbying and Antislavery in Congress." *Journal of the Early Republic* 33, no. 3 (2013): 523-547.

Congressional Globe, House of Representatives, 30th Congress, 1st session, 179.

Gates, Seth, to Giddings. December 5, 1848. Joshua Giddings Papers MSS 53, Box 3, Folder 4, #784, Ohio Connection, Columbus, Ohio.

Giddings, Joshua. *History of the Rebellion: Its Authors and Its Causes.* New York: Follett, Foster & Co, 1864. http://www.archive.org/details/historyofrebelli01gidd.

Giddings, Joshua, to Joseph Addison Giddings. August 13, 1843. Joshua Giddings Papers, MSS 53, Box 2, Folder 2, #339, Ohio Connection, Columbus, Ohio.

Green, Duff, to W.H. Williams. January 24, 1848. Duff Green Papers, Southern Historical Collection. Microfilm, reel 7, at Library of Congress, Washington, D.C.

Green, Fletcher M. "Duff Green, Militant Journalist of the Old School. *American Historical Review* 52, no. 2 (1947): 247–264.

Harrold, Stanley. *Subversives: Antislavery Community in Washington, DC, 1828–1865.* Baton Rouge: Louisiana State University, 2003.

Jacobs, Harriet. "Life Among the Contrabands." *Liberator.* September 5, 1862. http://www.docsouth.unc.edu/Jacobs and http://www.yale.edu/glc/harriet/12.htm.

Lincoln, Abraham, and Mary Todd, to Caleb. B. Smith. May 31, 1861. In the Abraham Lincoln Papers at the Library of Congress. Series 3. General correspondence. 1837–1897.

McIlvaine Papers, Wallace, Pennsylvania, Township.

National Era. "The Slave Case, Henry the Slave in Mrs. Sprigg's Boarding-house in Washington." February 24, 1848.

O'Brien, John. "Lincoln and the Abolitionists at the Sprigg House." *President Lincoln in Civil War Washington* (blog). Posted October 31, 2012. http://www.lincolninwashington.com/2012/10/3/lincoln-and-the-abolitionists-at-the-sprigg-house.

Pohl, Robert. "History: Lost Capitol Hill: Henry and Sylvia Wilson." *The Hillis Home* (blog). Posted May 22, 2017. http://www.TheHillisHome.com.

Schmidt, Sandra. "Ann Sprigg." *Bytes of History* (blog). http://bytesofhistory.org/Collections/UGRR/Sprigg_Ann _Ann-Biography.html.

Shelden, Rachel. "Messmates' Union: Friendship, Politics, and Living Arrangements in the Capital City, 1845–1861." *Journal of the Civil War Era* 1, no 4 (2011): 452–480.

ELS [Ezra L. Stevens]. "An Affecting Scene." *True Democrat*, February 28, 1848.

———. Editorial Correspondence: "Washington." *True Democrat*, February 15, 1848.

———. Editorial Correspondence: "Washington." *True Democrat*, February 16, 1848.

Stewart, James B. *Abolitionist Politics and the Coming of the Civil War.* Amherst: University of Massachusetts Press, 2008.

———. "Christian Statesmanship, Codes of Honor and Congressional Violence: The Antislavery Travails and Triumphs of Joshua Giddings." In Paul Finkelman and Donald R. Kennon, eds., *The Shadow of Freedom: The Politics of Slavery in the National Capital,* 36–57. Athens: Published for the United States Capitol Historical Society by Ohio University Press, 2011.

Wallach, Richard, to Duff Green. January 24, 1848. Duff Green Papers, Southern Historical Collection, University of North Carolina, Chapel Hill. Microfilm, reel 7, Library of Congress, Washington, D.C.

"Washington Correspondence." *True Democrat,* January 24, 1848.

Winkle, Kenneth J. *Lincoln's Citadel: The Civil War in Washington, DC.* New York: W.W. Norton, 2013.

William Chaplin

Canada West Census. 1861. Heads of Household.

The Case of William L. Chaplin: Being an Appeal to all Respecters of Law and Justice, Against the Cruel and Oppressive Treatment to Which, Under Color of Legal Proceedings, He Has Been Subjected, In the District of Columbia and Maryland. Boston Chaplin Committee, 1851. http://www.loc.gov/item/06043475.

Daily Union. No title. August 15, 1850.

Frederick Douglass Paper. "Address to Abolitionists in Respect of the Case of William L Chaplin." July 16, 1852.

———. "D.A. Hall Letter to William R. Smith." September 30, 1853.

———. "Gerrit Smith to William R. Smith Letter." July 23, 1852.

———. "Journal Sketches." June 26, 1851.

Harrold, Stanley. *Subversives: Antislavery Community in Washington, DC, 1828–1865.* Baton Rouge: Louisiana State University, 2003.

Liberty Party Paper. "William L. Chaplin." October 3, 1850.

National Era. "An Affray—The Arrest of William L. Chaplin." August 15, 1850.

———. "The Trial of W.L. Chaplin." November 21, 1850.

New National Era. No title. May 11, 1872.

New York Daily Times. No title. September 30, 1851.

New York Daily Tribune. "Case of W.L. Chaplin Bailed in Washington, But Imprisoned." September 23, 1850.

———. "From Washington." August 12, 1850.

———. "William Chaplin at Syracuse." January 11, 1851.

North Star. "Cazenovia Convention." September 5, 1850.

Ohio Census. 1863. Heads of Household.

Smith, Gerrit. "The Case of Chaplin." *New York Daily Times,* July 27, 1852.

Soderberg, Susan. "William Chaplin Arrest Site." Application, National Underground Railroad Network to Freedom. July 15, 2004.

U.S. Census. Heads of Household. 1880.

Garland H. White

Justice, George. "Robert Toombs (1810–1885)." *New Georgia Encyclopedia.* http://www.georgiaencyclopedia.org/articles/history.../robert-toombs-1810-1885.

Miller, Edward A., Jr. "Garland White, Black Army Chaplain." *Civil War History* 43 no. 3 (1997): 201–218.

National Independent Political Union [headed by Garland H White]. "Negro Declaration of Independence," February 28, 1876. Declaration Project. http://www.declarationproject.org.

New National Era. "Obituary." May 11, 1871.

Schwarz, Philip J. *Migrants Against Slavery: Virginians & the Nation.* Charlottesville: University Press of Virginia, 2001.

White, Garland H. "Execution of a Soldier." *Christian Recorder.* May 6, 1865.

———. "Help Us to Raise 10,000 Subscribers." *Christian Recorder.* October 1, 1864.

———. Letter. *Christian Recorder.* April 22, 1865. In Edwin Redkey, ed., *A Grand Army of Black Men.* Cambridge: Cambridge University Press, 1992.

———. Letter. *Christian Recorder.* August 8, 1864.

———. Letter. *Christian Recorder.* August 20, 1864.

———. Letter. *Christian Recorder.* March 15, 1865.

———. Letter. *Christian Recorder.* March 25, 1865.

———. Letter to Edwin M. Stanton. May 7, 1862. In Ira Berlin, Joseph P. Reidy and Leslie S. Rowland, eds. *Freedom: A Documentary History of Emancipation, 1861–1867,* Series 2, The Black Military Experience. Cambridge: Cambridge University Press, 1982.

———. Letter to Staunton and Seward. June 14, 1864. In Ira Berlin, Joseph P. Reidy and Leslie S. Rowland, eds. *Freedom: A Documentary History of Emancipation, 1861–1867,* Series 2, The Black Military Experience. Cambridge: Cambridge University Press, 1982.

————. Letter to W. Seward. May 18, 1864. Civil War Pensions Index. http://www.Fold3.com. Folder 3.

————. Letter to W. Seward. July 29, 1864. Civil War Pensions Index. http://www.Fold3.com.

————. Letter to W. Seward. [April] 1865. City Point, Virginia. Seward Papers, University of Rochester, Rochester, New York. In Peter C. Ripley, et al., *The Black Abolitionist Papers, 1830–1865*. Chapel Hill: University of North Carolina, microfilm.

————. Letter to William H. Seward. April 27, 1863. Seward Papers University of Rochester, Seward Paper, University of Rochester, Rochester, New York. In microfilm. In Peter C. Ripley, et al., *The Black Abolitionist Papers, 1830–1865*. Chapel Hill: University of North Carolina.

WHG [Garland H. White]. "An Interesting Letter from the 28th USCT." *Christian Recorder.* October 21, 1865.

————. Letter to editor. *Christian Recorder*. October 23, 1865.

Leonard Grimes

Brown, William Wells. *Black Man: His Antecedents, His Genius, and His Achievements*. New York: Krause Reprint Company, 1969. Reprint, New York: Thomas Hamilton; Boston: R.F. Wallcut, 1863. http://www.docsouth.unc.edu/neh/brownww/menu.html.

Campbell, Stanley W. *The Slave Catchers: Enforcement of the Fugitive Slave Law, 1850–1860*. Chapel Hill: University of North Carolina Press, 1968.

Certificate of Freedom. Loudoun County, Virginia. Leonard and Juliet Grimes. No. 545, 1826–01.

Collison, Gary. *Shadrach Minkins: From Fugitive Slave to Citizen*. Cambridge, MA: Harvard University Press, 1997.

Deed conveying 22nd and H St. property from Leonard Grimes to William Bush, Box 2 Folder 46, Georgetown University Library, Washington, D.C.

Emancipator. "From the Washington Globe '$700 Reward.'" December 5, 1839.

Genius of Liberty (Leesburg, Va). "Trial." March 14, 1840.

Hayden, Robert C. *Faith, Culture and Leadership: A History of the Black Church in Boston*. Boston: Boston Branch of the NAACP, 1983.

Higginson, Thomas Wentworth. *Cheerful Yesterdays*. New York: Arno Press, 1968 [reprint].

Jackson, Francis. Account Book of Francis Jackson, Treasurer, the Vigilance Committee of Boston. Boston: Bostonian Society [facsimile].

Jacobs, Donald M. *Courage and Conscience: Black and White Abolitionists in Boston*. Bloomington: Published for Boston Athenaeum by Indiana Press, 1993.

Lee, Deborah. "Leonard Andrew Grimes." In *The Essence of a People II: African Americans Who Made Their World Anew in Loudoun County, Virginia, and Beyond*, edited by Kendra Y. Hamilton, 21–25. Leesburg, VA: Black History Committee of the Friends of the Thomas Balch Library, 2002.

Levesque, George A. "Inherent Reformers—Inherited Orthodoxy: Black Baptists in Boston, 1800–1873." *Journal of Negro History* 60, no. 4 (1975): 491–525.

Levy, Leonard W. "Sims' Case: The Fugitive Slave Law in Boston in 1851." *Journal of Negro History* 35, no. 1 (1950): 39–74.

Loudoun County Miscellaneous Papers–Criminal, Leonard Grimes, Joseph Mead (owner) (crime: transporting slaves.)

Petition for Clemency for Leonard Grimes, Executive Papers of Governor Thomas W. Gilmer, 1840-Dec 3, Box 2, Folder 10, Library of Virginia, Richmond, Virginia.

Petition 20484001. Records of the U.S. District Court, Segregated Habeas Corpus, February 13, 1840, Box 1, Folder 28, National Archives, Washington, D.C. http://www.library.uncg.edu/slavery/permission.

Schwartz, Harold. "Fugitive Slave Days in Boston." *New England Quarterly* 27, no. 2 (1954): 191–212.

Schwarz, Philip. Unpublished Notes on Leonard Grimes." Thomas Balch Library, Leesburg, Virginia.

Simmons, William J. *Men of Mark: Eminent, Progressive, and Rising*. Cleveland, OH: George M. Rewell, 1891. http://www.docsouth.unc.edu/neh/simmons/menu.html.

Stevens, Charles Emery. *Anthony Burns: A History*. Boston: J.P. Hewett & Company, 1856. http://www.doc.south.unc.edu/neh/stevens/stevens.html.

U.S. Census, Heads of Household. 1840–1890.

Woodson, Carter G. *The History of the Negro Church*. Washington, D.C.: Carter Godwin Woodson Association Publishers, 2nd ed. 1921.

John Dean

Baltimore Sun. "An Important Fugitive Slave Case." June 14, 1862.

———. "Conflict Between the Civil and Military Authorities of Washington." May 24, 1862.

———. "Fugitive Slave Excitement in Washington." May 23, 1862.

———. "The Copeland Fugitive Slave Case." May 30, 1862.

———. "The Fugitive Slave Case." May 12, 1863.

———. "The Fugitive Slave Case." May 21, 1863.

———. "The Fugitive Slave Case." May 25, 1863.

———. "The Fugitive Slave Case—The Court Decided on the Subject— The Negro Discharged." May 23, 1863.

———. "The Fugitive Slave Commissioner." May 28, 1863.

Brooklyn Daily Eagle. "An Old Brooklynite Gone." October 17, 1863.

Civil War Pensions Index. Colored Infantry. Andrew Hall, Co. D, 1st Regiment. http://www.Fold3.com.

Court Slave Records for the District of Columbia. Fugitive Slave Cases. John Jackson and Bill Jackson. http://www.Fold3.com.

Daily Advertiser. "From Washington." May 29, 1862.

Daily National Intelligencer. "The Fugitive Slave Case." June 9, 1863.

Dean, John. Letter to H.R. Dean. June 7, 1862. Dean Family Papers, Indiana Historical Society, Indianapolis, Indiana. Transcription in Sandra Schmidt Notes.

———. Letter to H.R. Dean. June 15, 1862. Dean Family Papers, Indiana Historical Society, Indianapolis, Indiana. Transcription in Sandra Schmidt Notes.

———. Letter to Mary Dean. May 14, 1863. Dean Family Papers, Indiana Historical Society, Indianapolis, Indiana. Transcription in Sandra Schmidt Notes.

———. Letter to H.R. Dean. May 25, 1863. Dean Family Papers, Indiana Historical Society, Indianapolis, Indiana. Transcription in Sandra Schmidt Notes.

———. Letter to H.R. Dean. June 3, 1863. Dean Family Papers, Indiana Historical Society, Indianapolis, Indiana. Transcription in Sandra Schmidt Notes.

———. Letter to H.R. Dean. June 18, 1863. Dean Family Papers, Indiana Historical Society, Indianapolis, Indiana. Transcription in Sandra Schmidt Notes.

Evening Star. "Fugitive Slave Case." June 13, 1862.

———. "The Funeral of Mr. Dean." October 17, 1863.

Logic, Bob. "Letter from Washington," *Anglo-American*. August 1, 1863.

Mackey, Franklin H., reported by. "In Re Andrew Hall." In *District of Columbia Supreme Court Reports* 6 (1889): 10ff. Buffalo, NY: Dennis & Company, 1951 [reprint].

Mulderink, Earl. *New Bedford's Civil War*. New York: Fordham University, 2012.

Morris, Jeffrey Brandon. *Calmly to Poise the Scales of Justice*. Durham, NC: Carolina Academic Press, 2001.

National Republican. "An Exciting Fugitive Slave." May 22, 1862.

———. "The Fugitive Slave Case—Decision of the Commissioners—The Slave Given Up to His Master." May 23, 1862.

———. "Fugitive Slave Case Still Unsettled." May 23, 1863.

———. "Trouble in Arresting Fugitive Slaves." May 23, 1862.

New York Daily Tribune. "Kidnapping in Washington." May 30, 1863.

Schmidt, Sandra. "The Defense of Fugitive Slaves in DC—1862–1863." Paper presented at the D.C. History Conference, Washington, D.C., November 2013.

———. "John Dean." *Bytes of History* (blog). http://www.bytesofhistory.org/Collections/UGRR/Dean_John/Dean_John-Biography.html.

———. Unpublished Notes on Dean papers, John Dean Diary and Letters.

Tarter, John. "John C. Underwood, 1809–1873." *Encyclopedia of Virginia Biography*. http://www.encyclopediavirginia.org/Underwood_John_C_1809–1873.

Yardley Taylor

Crothers, A. Glenn. *Quakers Living in the Lion's Mouth: The Society of Friends in Northern Virginia, 1730–1865*. Gainesville: University Press of Florida, 2012.

Lawrence, Lee. "From the Archives: Loudoun Slavery and Three Brave Men." *Loudoun Now*, October 26, 2017.

Taylor Family Papers, 1817–1872 (SC 0097). Thomas Balch Library, Leesburg, Virginia.

Taylor, Yardley. Letter to Cyrus Griest. October 2, 1875. Albert Cook Myers Papers, Chester County Historical Society, West Chester, Pennsylvania.

"Verdict on Yardley Taylor." Virginia Tenth Judicial Circuit, Loudoun County, Virginia. February 22, 1830.

William Boyd

Evening Star. "The Case of Boyd." November 19, 1858.

———. "Dr. Boyd, The Slave Abductor." November 21, 1858.

———. "Dr. W. Boyd—Another Osawatomie Brown on a Small Scale." November 10, 1858.

———. "Dr. Wm. Boyd." November 15, 1858.

———. "Honorably Dismissed." November 22, 1858.

———. "Today—Wm. Boyd." January 13, 1859.

Schmidt, Sandra. "Dr. William Boyd." *Bytes of History* (blog). http://www.bytesofhistory.org/Collections/UGRR/Boyd_William-Biography.html.

———. "William Boyd and D.A. Hall Burial Sites." Application, National Underground Railroad Network to Freedom. January 5, 2010.

INDEX

ABOUT THE AUTHOR

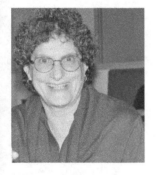

Jenny Masur is a native Washingtonian. She worked for seventeen years for the National Park Service as National Capital Regional Manager for the National Underground Railroad Network to Freedom. Her doctorate is in anthropology, and her interest in individual lives dates from the oral history she co-edited while in graduate school. Her respect for the heroes of the Underground Railroad continues to grow.